CANDLESTICK PATTERNS CRASH COURSE

prt

PUSHKAR RAJ THAKUR

For permissions, contact:
Invincible Publication Pvt. Ltd.
201A, SAS Tower, Sector 38, Gurugram - 122003
Phone: +91-124-4034247
www.invinciblepublishers.com

Sales Office: -4760-61/23, Basement, Pratap Street,
Ansari Road, Daryaganj, New Delhi - 110002
Email: invinciblepublishers@gmail.com

Title: Candlestick Patterns Crash Course
Author: Pushkar Raj Thakur
ISBN: 978-93-5886-823-4

Printed in India
First Edition: October, 2024

1.

Introduction

1. So जब कोई beginner stock market के technical language को सुनता है, जैसे "price action" या फिर "candlestick analysis", तो वो कुछ स्टार्ट करने से पहले ही हार मान लेता है।

2. People often feel intimidated by this vocabulary and this is why they enter trading without understanding how the market works, how trends work and how these trends are analyzed.

3. Especially when it comes to the charts and graphs, लोग totally skip कर देते हैं उन्हें देखना, क्योंकि वे confused हो जाते हैं या इतनी information और statistics से overwhelm (अभिभूत) हो जाते हैं। And this is why we have created this book.

WHAT IS THE UNDER CANDLESTICK

NEED TO STAND PATTERNS?

Whenever you make an investment or you trade in the stock market, you are required to conduct fundamental and technical analysis. Candlestick chart pattern इसी technical analysis का एक हिस्सा (part) है, जिसके through आप market की movement को predict कर सकते हो।

LINE CHART

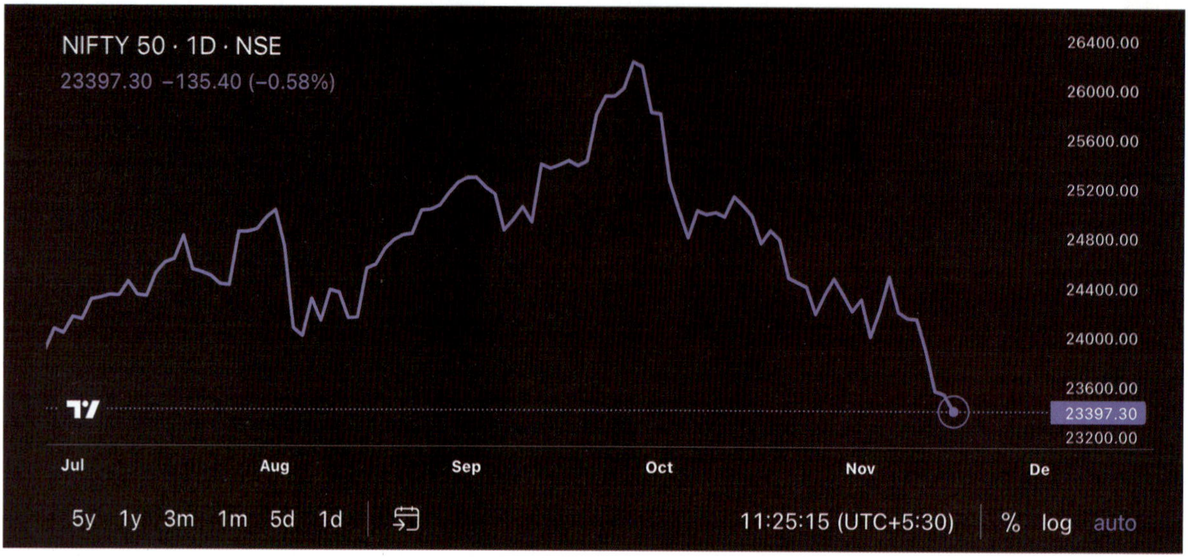

CANDLESTICK CHART

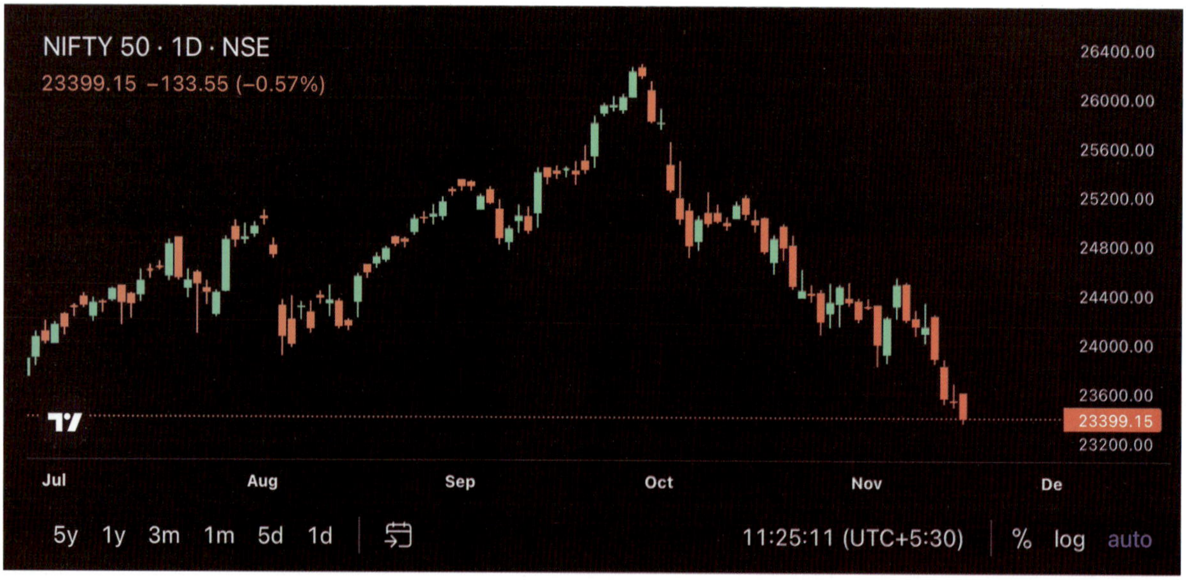

Look at these charts. Which one appears to be simpler to understand? इन दोनों में से आपको कौन-सा chart simple लग रहा है समझने में?

I think for most people it will be the first one. पहला chart सिर्फ एक line दिखाता है और दूसरा chart बहुत सारी candlesticks को।

इसी चीज़ की वजह से बहुत सारे लोग candlestick chart pattern को overlook कर देते हैं because they appear to be really complex.

However, in this book I have simplified these patterns for you so that आप technical analysis (टेक्निकल एनालिसिस) को अपने favour में use कर पाओ।

Before we dive deeper into the topic let us first understand

CANDLESTICKS

आखिर होती क्या है?

WHAT ARE CANDLESTICKS?

Stock Market में candlesticks एक बहुत important technical analysis का tool है, जो traders को market के behavior को समझने में मदद करता है। Candlesticks का use करते हुए, traders market के price movement को visualize कर पाते हैं। Candlesticks chart पर हर candlestick एक specific time period को represent करता है, जिसमें stock के opening, closing, high और low prices दर्शाई जाती हैं। हर candlestick के colors और shapes अलग होते हैं और इनकी study करके traders market trend, volatility (अस्थिरता) और reversal को predict करते हैं।

To sum it up, candlesticks are visual representations of 4 main things in a given time period, i.e- open, close, high and low price.

STRUCTURE OF A CANDLESTICK

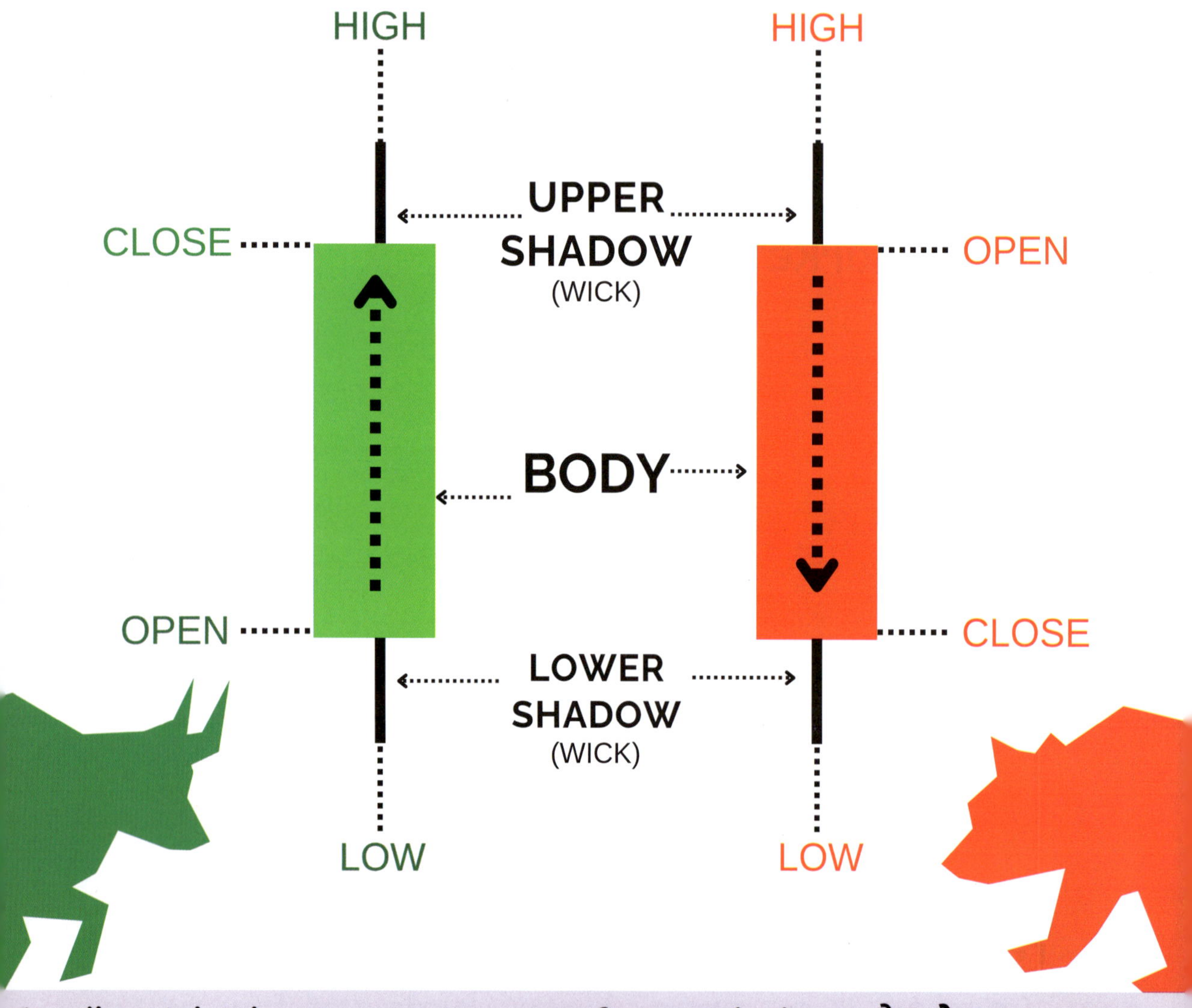

Candlestick charts एक type का financial chart है जो securities, derivatives, और currencies के price movements को describe करते हैं। हर candlestick एक specific time period को represent करता है और चार crucial pieces of information दिखाता है: opening price, closing price, highest price, और lowest price.

BODY

REAL BODY

1. Open Price: ये वो price है जहां stock ने specific time period के लिए trading start की।

2. Close Price: ये वो price है जहां stock ने specific time period के लिए trading end की।

3. Body: Ye rectangular part होता है candlestick ka, jo opening और closing prices के बीच का range represent करता है।

4. Green/White Body: अगर close price higher है open price से, तो candlestick usually green या white होता है, जो bullish sentiment (price increased during the period) को indicate करता है।

5. Red/Black Body: अगर close price lower है open price से, तो candlestick usually red या black होता है, जो bearish sentiment (price decreased during the period) को indicate करता है।

WICKS (SHADOWS):

- Upper Wick (Upper Shadow): ये line body के ऊपर होती है, जो highest price during the period ko represent करती है।
- Lower Wick (Lower Shadow): ये line body के neeche होती है, जो lowest price during the period ko represent करती है।
- Wicks price extremes (highs and lows) को show करते हैं time period के दौरान।

Why Candle is Green or Red ?

Green Candle (Bullish Candle)	Red Candle (Bearish Candle)
• Explanation: एक green candlestick तब बनता है जब closing price higher होता है opening price से। यह indicate करता है कि asset का price trading period के दौरान increase हुआ।	• Explanation: एक red candlestick तब बनता है जब closing price lower होता है opening price से। यह indicate करता है कि asset का price trading period के दौरान decrease हुआ।
• Market Sentiment: ये signify करता है कि buyers sellers से ज़्यादा dominant थे, जिसकी वजह से asset का price rise हुआ।	• Market Sentiment: यह signify करता है कि sellers buyers से ज़्यादा dominant थे, जिसकी वजह से asset का price decline हुआ।
• Visual Cue: Green color often growth या positivity se associated होता है, इसलिए upward price movements को represent करने के लिए intuitive होता है।	• Visual Cue: Red color often danger या negativity से associated होता है, इसलिए downward price movements को represent करने के लिए intuitive होता है।

COLOURS OF CANDLESTICKS

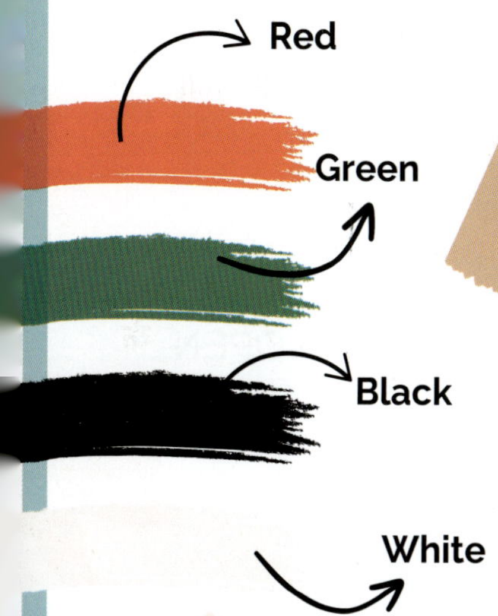

4 type के colors, red, green, black and white में generally candlesticks होती है। White और black candlesticks पहले forex market में use हुआ करती थी लेकिन अब red and green होती हैं, where black=red and white=green.

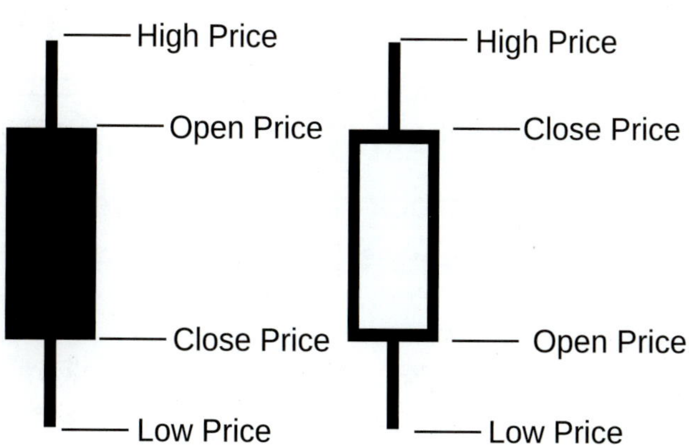

Green candlesticks market में bullish (upward trend) trend और Red candlestick bearish trend (downward trend) को दर्शाता हैं। जब stock price trading session के दौरान ऊपर जाता है तो green candlesticks दिखाई देते हैं, जबकि नीचे जाता है तो red.

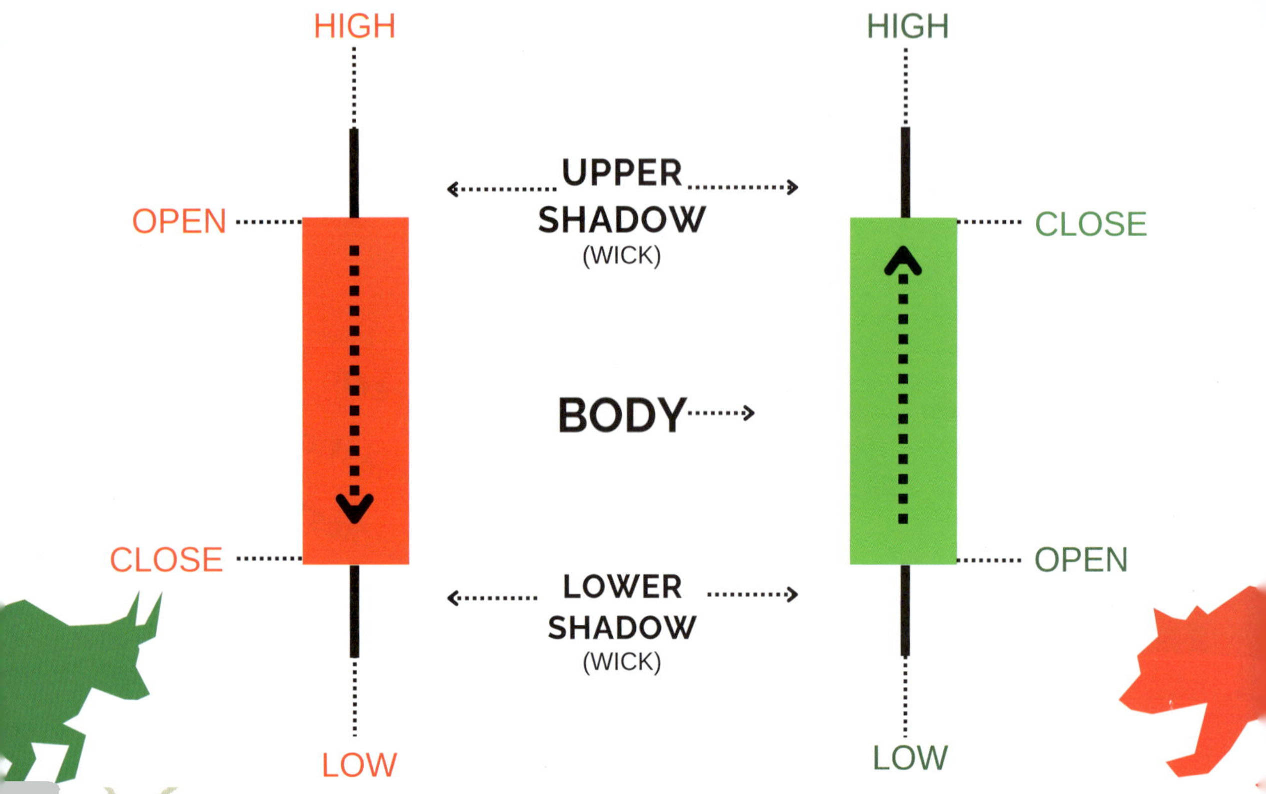

चलिए एक example के साथ समझते हैं। मान लीजिए कि एक stock का current price ₹ 100 है और आपको एक candlestick chart देखने को मिलता है जिसमें एक green candle दिख रहा है।

- इस green candle का open price ₹100 और close price ₹115 है।
- इसका मतलब है कि stock के price ने trading session के दौरान बढ़ना शुरू किया (open price ₹100). इसका highest price ₹130 गया और lowest price ₹95. पर session के end में stock ₹115 पर close हुआ।
- यह दिखाता है कि traders के ज़्यादातर buyers थे और stock का price बढ़ गया।
- इस green candle को देखकर, traders को लग सकता है कि market में bullish sentiment है और अगले कुछ समय में price और बढ़ सकती है।

अब, अगर एक red candle होता तो:

- इस red candle का open price ₹100 और close price ₹90 है।
- इसका मतलब है कि stock ke price में trading session के दौरान गिरावट आई (open price ₹100). इसका highest price ₹110 गया और lowest price ₹85. पर session के end में stock ₹90 पर close हुआ।
- ये दिखाता है कि traders के ज़्यादातर sellers थे और stock का price गिर गया।
- Is red candle को देखकर, traders को लग सकता है कि market में bearish sentiment है और अगले कुछ समय में price और नीचे जा सकता है।

तो, Candlestick charts के patterns का मतलब समझना बारिश की prediction करने जैसा है। जैसे बादल का color और state बारिश को predict करने में मदद करते हैं। वैसे ही candlestick charts के patterns market की movement को समझाने में मदद करते हैं। Candlestick charts के patterns का analysis करना एक खतरनाक कुत्ते से बचने जैसा भी है। जैसे लोग एक पागल कुत्ते से गुज़रते वक्त अपनी protection करते हैं, या रास्ता बदल लेते हैं, वैसे ही traders candlestick patterns को analyze करते हैं ताकि market के risks और movements को समझ पाएं और सही decision ले सकें।

जब candlestick pattern की बात आती है तो ये जानना important है कि a pattern can be formed with any number of candles. A single candle can also signify a pattern. Two candles can also create a pattern and so on. To keep things simple, we will start with single candlestick patterns first.

NOTES

NOTES

To Open Free Demat Account, Just Scan the QR Code

2.

Single candlestick patterns

देखो candlesticks patterns का बनना generally trend reversal को indicate करता है। And trend reversal को समझने के लिए हमें पहले trend को समझना पड़ेगा।

Q WHAT IS TREND?

Trend का मतलब है market का general direction. Trend को समझने का simple तरीका है कि chart पर price के movements को देखो। अगर price generally ऊपर जा रहे हैं, तो उस trend को "uptrend" कहते हैं। और अगर price नीचे जा रहे हैं, तो उस ट्रेंड को "downtrend" कहते हैं।

अगर prices कहीं भी बिना किसी clear direction के हैं, मतलब zig-zag manner में ऊपर-नीचे हो रहा हैं, तो उसको "sideways" trend कहते हैं।

अब जहाँ candlestick pattern आ जाता है वहाँ बहुत zyada chances होते हैं कि trend reverse हो जाए। हम एक-एक करके इन patterns को समझते हैं।

Note: colour of the candlestick doesn't matter while analyzing the trends using these patterns

HAMMER AND HANGING MAN

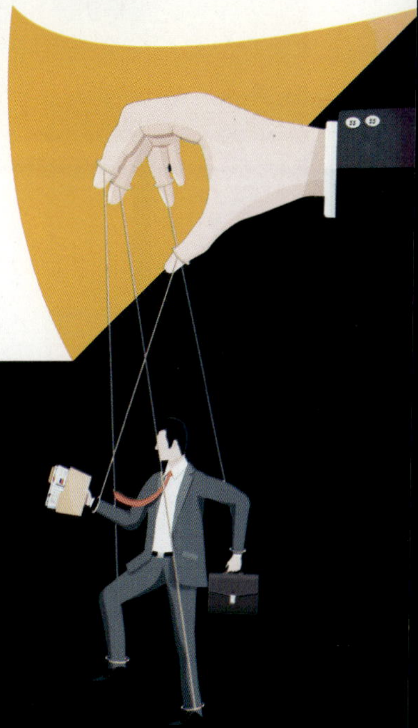

PATTERN 1

Hammer

जब एक stock के candlestick chart में ऐसे pattern आते हैं जिसमें एक candlestick की छोटी body होती है और उस body के मुकाबले 3 times बड़ी shadow नीचे की तरफ होती है, और एक बहुत छोटी सी shadow ऊपर की तरफ होती है तो वहाँ hammer pattern बनता है।

Hammer pattern का matlab होता है कि market में sell-off हुआ था पर फिर से buyers ने control ले लिया है। समझो जैसे hammer से छोटे-छोटे nail मारकर कुछ pattern या form बनाया जाता है, वैसे ही traders hammer pattern देखकर समझ जाते हैं कि chances है कि stock ke price me ऊपर की direction में move aaskta hai.

HAMMER

Hanging Man

जब एक छोटी सी candlestick chart में एक लंबी छोटी body हो और ऊपर एक छोटा सा shadow (छाया) होता है, और नीचे की तरफ एक लंबी सी shadow हो at least 3 times of the body तो वो hanging man pattern कहलाता है।

Hanging man pattern ka मतलब होता है कि market में initially buyers control में थे, पर फिर sell-off हुआ है। इस pattern को देखकर traders को लगता है कि अब price में नीचे का movement होने वाला है। जैसे कि hanging man लटके हुए होते हैं, वैसे ही hanging man pattern देखकर traders थोड़ा alert हो जाते हैं।

HANGING MAN

WHAT HAPPENS WHEN YOU SEE THESE PATTERNS ON A CHART?

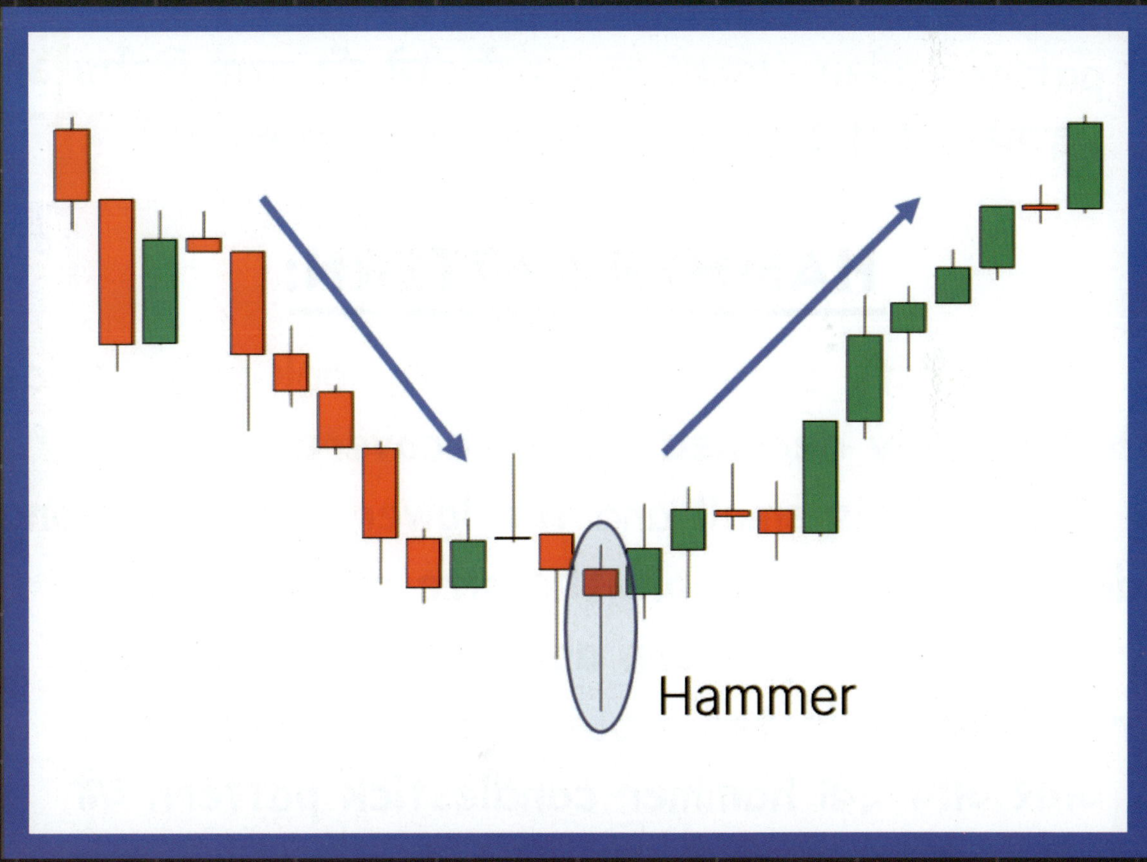

1. HAMMER

जब आप chart पर hammer pattern देखते हैं, तो ये एक indication हो सकता है कि market का direction बदलने वाला है। Hammer pattern एक bullish reversal pattern होता है, मतलब जब market downtrend से uptrend में बदलने की possibility होती है।

Hammer pattern का structure simple होता है - एक छोटी सी body होती है और लंबी lower wick, यह candle को एक hammer जैसा look देता है।

ये pattern हमेशा आपको chart में नीचे की तरफ मिलेगा और इसकेआने पे एक upward movement start होती है।

HAMMER PATTERN:

- To identify a hammer pattern, look for a price that initially declined, then recovered.
- The body is small and the lower shadow is long, ideally double or triple the size of the body.
- The hammer pattern appears in a downward trend and indicates a potential trend reversal.
- अगर आप एक hammer candlestick pattern को confirm करना चाहते हैं, तो next day confirmation candlestick का इंतज़ार करें।

When to enter?

Let's assume the following:

- Stock XYZ is trading at ₹50.
- The hammer candlestick forms, with the low of the candlestick reaching ₹48 and the close at ₹49.

In this scenario, you might consider entering the trade if the price moves above the high of the hammer candlestick. Let's say the high of the hammer candlestick is ₹49.50.

You decide to enter the trade if the price reaches ₹49.60. This confirms that the buyers are taking control and the bullish reversal might be in progress. So, you enter the trade at ₹49.60.

Now, let's determine the stop loss. A common approach is to set the stop loss just below the low of the hammer candlestick to protect against potential losses if the reversal doesn't materialize.

2. HANGING MAN

जब आप chart पर hanging मैन pattern देखते हैं, तो ये एक bearish reversal signal हो सकता है. Hanging man pattern usually uptrend के end को indicate करता है और potential trend reversal को suggest करता है।

Hanging man pattern का structure एक लंबी lower wick और chhoti सी body होती है। यह pattern hanging man की तरह resemble करता है। वैसे तो hammer और hanging man दोनों एक जैसे दिखते हैं, लेकिन इनके effect और position की वजह से इनके नाम अलग-अलग हैं।

Traders को इस signal को समझकर caution और risk management maintain करना चाहिए। इसका मतलब है कि long positions (buying positions) लेना कम कर देना चाहिए या फिर stop-loss levels को tighten करना चाहिए।

यह candlestick patterns की study Japan से shuru हुई थी, जहां traders ने उन्हें पहचान कर trading strategies (ट्रेडिंग रणनीतियाँ) develop की। इसी कारण इन patterns के Japanese names हैं, जैसे कि "hammer" और "hanging man".

HANGING MAN PATTERN:

To identify a hanging man pattern, look for a price that initially rose, then moved downward.

The body is small and the lower shadow is long, ideally double or triple the size of the body.

The hanging man pattern appears in an upward trend and indicates a potential trend reversal.

अगर आप एक hanging man candle-stick pattern को confirm करना चाहते हैं,तो next day एक confirmation candlestick का wait करें।

LET'S ASSUME THE FOLLOWING:

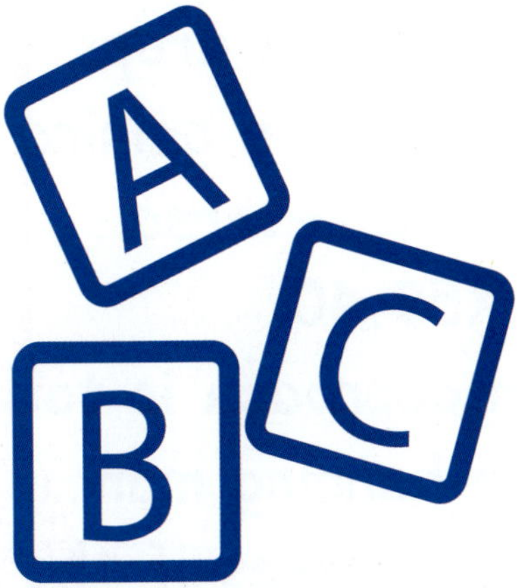

Stock ABC is trading at ₹60.

The hanging man candlestick forms, with the high of the candlestick reaching ₹62 and the close at ₹61.

Now, for entering the trade and setting the stop loss: You might consider entering the trade if the price falls below the low of the hanging man candlestick. Let's say the low of the hanging man candlestick is ₹59.50.

You decide to enter the trade if the price drops to₹59.40. This confirms that the sellers are gaining control, potentially indicating a bearish reversal.

So, you enter the trade at ₹59.40.

For setting the stop loss, a common approach is to place it just above the high of the hanging man candlestick to protect against potential losses if the reversal doesn't occur.

In our example, the high of the hanging man candlestick is ₹62. Therefore, you might set your stop loss at ₹62.10 to provide some buffer room and avoid getting stopped out due to minor fluctuations.

Color does not matter because their shape is exactly the same and it is the position(whether it appears in downtrend or uptrend) of this candlestick that indicates the market movement.

FIRST STOCK EXCHANGE IN ASIA:

The Bombay Stock Exchange (BSE), established in 1875, is Asia's oldest stock exchange and was initially just a small group of stock brokers who met under a banyan tree in Mumbai.

ACTIVITY TIME

How many Time did a hammer candlestick pattern form in Nifty 50 Chart from Nov 2023 to 31 oct 2024 on Daily Times Frame ?

- 1
- 3
- 5
- 4

INVERTED HAMMER & SHOOTING STAR

PATTERN 2

जब छोटी rectangular body के साथ ऊपर की तरफ एक बड़ी shadow बनती है और नीचे ki तरफ एक बहुत ही छोटी सी shadow बनती है तो उसका significance और indication change हो जाता है। जब ये bullish trend को indicate करे तो उसे inverted Hammer कहते हैं। जब ये bearish trend को indicate करे तो उसे Shooting Star कहते हैं।

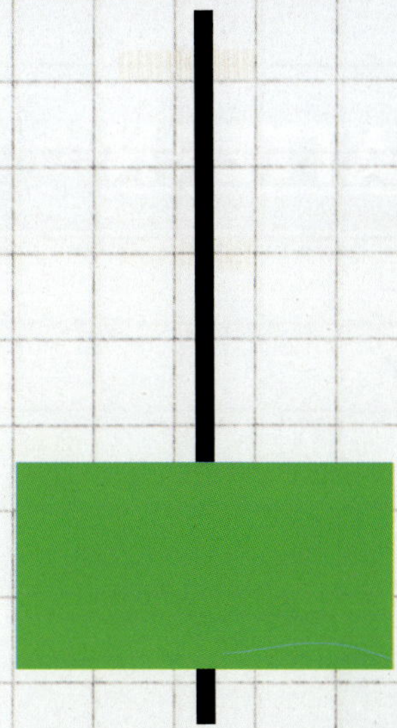

INVERTED HAMMER

इसमें, candle की body छोटी होती है और ऊपर shadow जो highest price को indicate करती है वो long होती है, appearing like an inverted hammer. ये pattern तब दिखता है जब price पहले गिरती है और फिर ऊपर चढ़ता है लेकिन close price, open price के थोड़ा पास ही आकर रुकता है। यह downward trend के बाद आता है और trend का reversal indicate करता है।

Shooting star pattern में candle की body छोटी होती है और ऊपर shadow बड़ी होती है, जिससे ये एक shooting star की तरह लगता है। ये pattern तब दिखता है जब price पहले ऊपर जाता है और फिर नीचे आता है, और close price, open price से नीचे होता है। ये upward trend के बाद आता है और trend का reversal indicate करता है। और क्योंकि ये bearish trend indicate करता है, तो ये हमेशा upward trend में ही आता है, मतलब chart के ऊपर की तरफ।

SHOOTING STAR

INVERTED HAMMER PATTERN

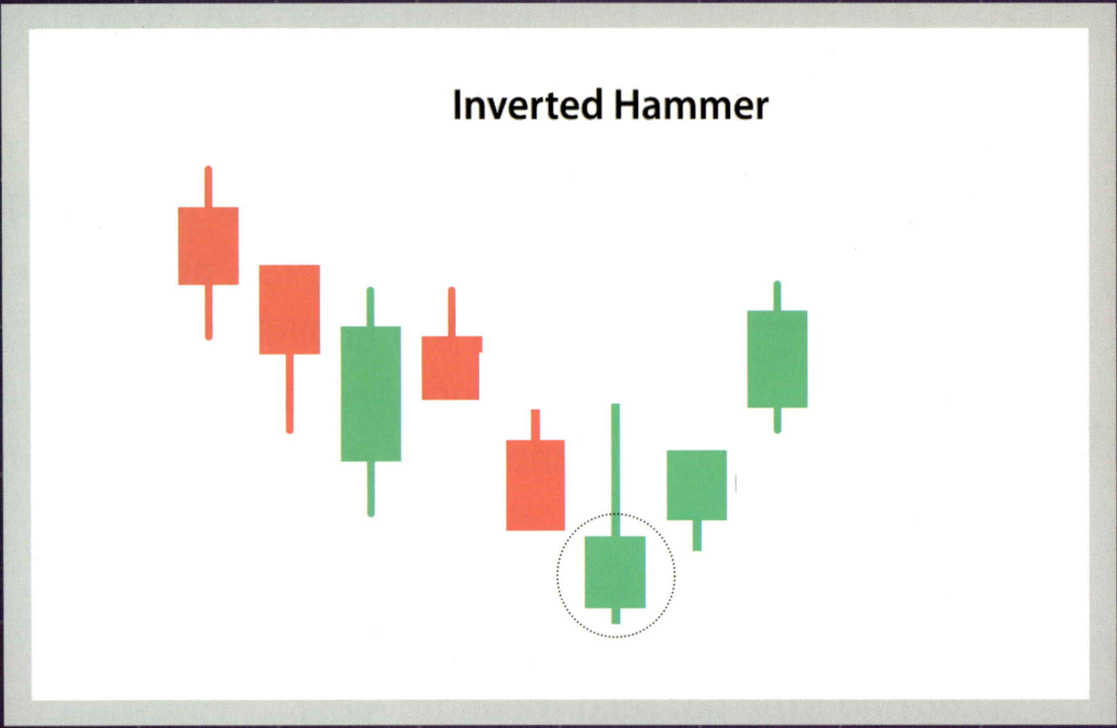

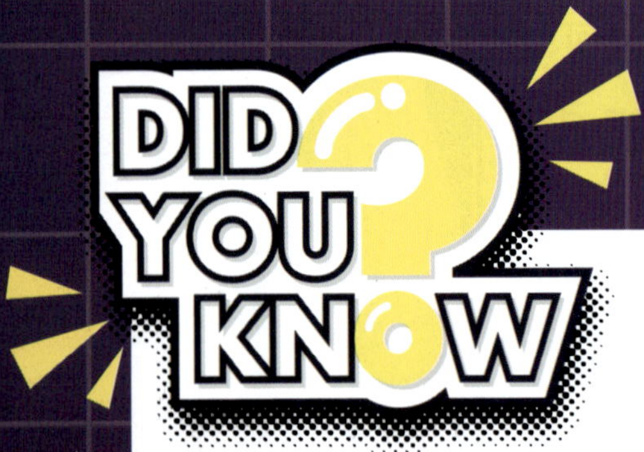

The inverted hammer candlestick pattern often signals a potential reversal in a downtrend. Despite its name, it appears at the bottom of a downward price movement, indicating that buyers are starting to gain strength. When confirmed by subsequent bullish candles, it can suggest a shift in market sentiment and a possible trend reversal!

SHOOTING STAR

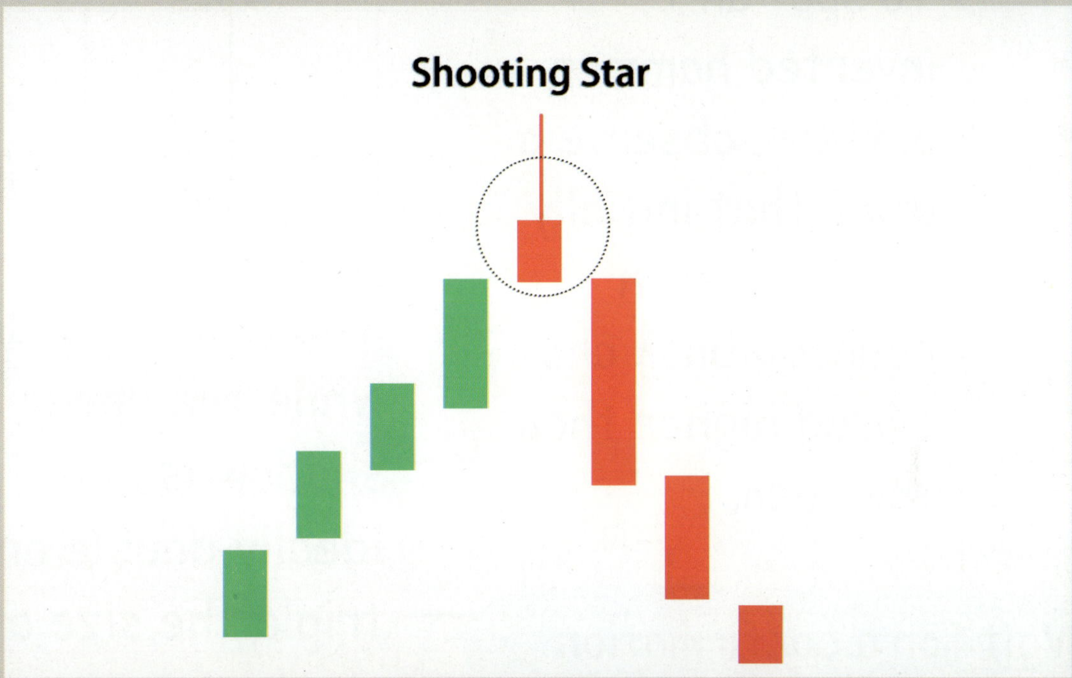

DID YOU KNOW?

The shooting star candlestick pattern typically appears at the top of an uptrend and signals a potential reversal. It has a small body and a long upper shadow, indicating that buyers pushed the price higher, but sellers stepped in, driving the price back down. When confirmed by bearish candles following its formation, it suggests that the upward momentum may be weakening!

INVERTED HAMMER PATTERN

To spot an inverted hammer pattern, observe a price that initially declined, then bounced back and closed higher than the open.

The body is small, while the upper shadow is long, ideally double or triple the size of the body.

Wait for a confirmation candlestick on the following trading day. Ideally, the next candlestick should open higher (bullish gap-up) or close above the high of the Inverted Hammer candlestick, indicating continued bullish momentum.

This pattern typically appears in a downtrend and suggests a possible reversal in the trend.

SHOOTING STAR PATTERN

- To identify a shooting star pattern, watch for a price that initially rose, then dropped and closed lower than the open.

- The body is small, and the upper shadow is long, ideally double or triple the size of the body.

- The shooting star pattern occurs after an upward trend and indicates a potential reversal in the trend.

- Wait for a confirmation candlestick on the following trading day. Ideally, the next candlestick should open lower (bearish gap-down) or close below the low of the Shooting Star candlestick, indicating continued bearish momentum.

WHERE TO ENTER *and* EXIT ?

1 EXAMPLE

मान लीजिए आपको एक share के daily chart पर एक inverted hammer candlestick pattern दिखाई देता है jiski Opening price ₹60 है, दिन के Trading Session ke दौरान price सबसे ज़्यादा ₹62 है, सबसे कम price ₹58 है, और closing price ₹61 है।

1. To start Trading watch for open on Next day:

- Inverted hammer pattern बनने और बंद होने का wait करें।
- अगले candle के opening price पर trade शुरू करें, जो कि ₹61 हो सकता है या थोड़ा सा ज़्यादा ताकि bullish momentum confirm हो सके।

2. Stop Loss Set करने का price:

- Inverted hammer candle की low के नीचे stop-loss order रखें, जो ₹58 है।
- उदाहरण के तौर पर, आप stop loss को ₹57.50 पर set कर सकते हैं, थोड़ा buffer देना है low के नीचे।

तो, इस example में:

- Open price शुरू करने का: ₹61 (या थोड़ा सा ज़्यादा)
- Stop Loss: ₹57.50

2 EXAMPLE

मान लीजिए आपको एक share के daily chart पर एक shooting star candlestick pattern दिखाई देता है। Opening price ₹70 है, दिन के दौरान सबसे ज़्यादा price ₹72 है, sabse कम price ₹68 है, और closing price ₹71 है।

1. Trading शुरू करने के लिए open price:

- Shooting star pattern बनने और बंद होने का wait करें।
- Agla candle का opening price से थोड़ा नीचे trade शुरू करें, जो कि ₹70 हो सकता है या थोड़ा सा कम।

2. Stop Loss Set करने का price:

- Shooting star candle की high के ऊपर stop-loss order रखें, जो ₹72 है।
- उदाहरण के तौर पर, aap stop loss को ₹72.50 पर set kar सकते हैं, थोड़ा buffer देना है high के ऊपर।

तो, इस example में:

- **Open price शुरू करने का: ₹70 (या थोड़ा सा कम)**
- **Stop Loss: ₹72.50**

ये levels भी आपके risk management और trade strategy के हिसाब से adjust किए जा सकते हैं।

THE ROLE OF HARSHAD MEHTA:

Harshad Mehta's stock market scandal in the early 1990s was one of India's largest financial frauds. This led to massive regulatory reforms, including the formation of the Securities and Exchange Board of India (SEBI) to oversee and regulate market operations more strictly.

ACTIVITY TIME

On November 30, 2018, a shooting star Candlestick Pattern Appeared on the Daily Chart of Reliance Industries. What was the subsequent Price Movement after that?

- Corrected 5%
- Corrected 3.5%
- Corrected 7.8%
- Corrected 9.39%

DRAGONFLY DOJI & GRAVESTONE DOJI

PATTERN 3

Dragonfly doji single candlestick pattern है जो technical analysis में use होता है। इस pattern में candlestick की body बिल्कुल छोटी होती है और lower wick body के comparison (तुलना) में 5 times longer होता है जबकि upper wick या तो negligible (नगण्य) होता है या फिर बिल्कुल नहीं होता।

Dragonfly doji pattern का matlab होता है कि market में confusion है या फिर indecision है। इसका मतलब ये भी होता है कि sellers ने काफी ज़ोर लगाया जिससे पहले price नीचे push हुआ पर फिर buyers ने भी equal ज़ोर लगाया और close price, open price के बिल्कुल पास but ऊपर आकर रुक गया, जिससे body बिल्कुल छोटी सी बनती है लेकिन lower price की wick बहुत लंबी बनती है। इसमें buyers dominant होती है और वो control में होते हैं।

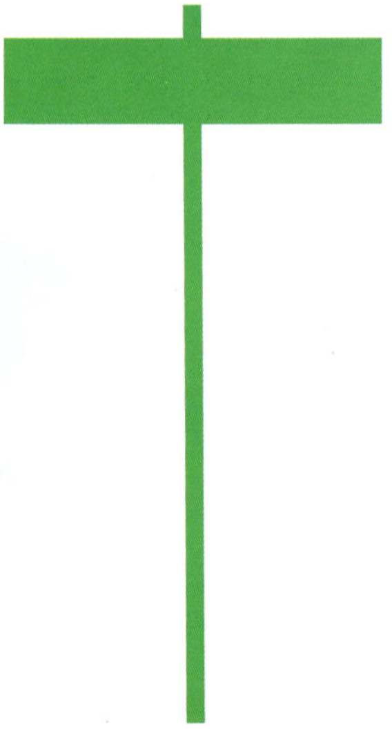

DRAGONFLY DOJI

Assume the following scenario:

DRAGONFLY DOJI

- Stock XYZ is currently trading at ₹100.
- A Dragonfly Doji forms, with the opening price at ₹100, the low at ₹70, and the closing price at ₹105.
- The next candle opens at ₹105 and closes at ₹115.

For the Dragonfly Doji:

- Entry Price: Since the Dragonfly Doji indicates potential bullish reversal, a trader might consider first confirming the trend by observing the next candlestick. The closing price of this candle should be higher than dragonfly doji candle. And if it does, you can enter the buy trade by placing entry on the closing price of this candlestick. So, let's say the entry price is set at ₹115.
- Stop Loss: To manage risk, a stop-loss order can be placed below the low of the Dragonfly Doji. So, let's set the stop-loss price at ₹70.

इसका structure एक cross की तरह भी लगता है। इस pattern को देखकर traders को ये समझ आता है कि buyers और sellers के बीच में कुछ balance या equilibrium है। जब एक dragonfly doji candlestick pattern market में दिखता है, traders इसे future price movement का indication समझते हैं। अगर ये pattern downtrend के बाद aata है तो ये bullish reversal का sign हो sakta है और अगर इसका inverted structure uptrend के बाद आ जाए तो इसका नाम change हो जाता है और तब ये कहलाता है Gravestone Doji.

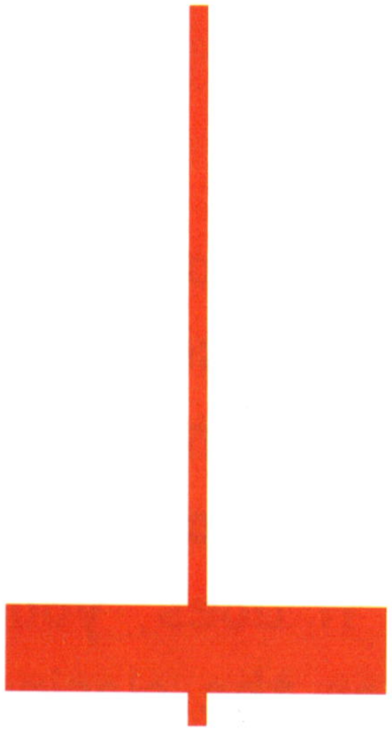

GRAVESTONE DOJI

Gravestone doji single candlestick pattern है। इस pattern में candlestick की body बिल्कुल छोटी-सी होती है, just like the Dragonfly Doji लेकिन, ये inverted होता है और इसका upper wick body के comparison में 5 times longer होता है जबकि lower wick या तो बहुत छोटा होता है या फिर बिल्कुल नहीं होता। Gravestone doji pattern को नाम उसकी appearance से मिलता है, जिसमें candle की shape gravestone जैसी दिखती है। इस pattern को देखकर traders को ये समझ आता है कि market में सेलर्स का dominance है और price काफी नीचे जाने की possibility है।

जब gravestone doji candlestick pattern market में dikhta है, traders इसे bearish reversal का sign समझते हैं, मतलब अगर uptrend था तो अब market की direction downward जाने की possibility है।

इससे पता चलता है कि buyers पहले पूरा effort लगाते हैं to drive the price upwards लेकिन फिर sellers dominant हो जाते हैं और price को नीचे की तरफ push कर देते है and they close price below the open price.

Gravestone Doji जब भी बनता है आपको chart में ये एक black cross जैसा भी नज़र आ सकता है।

Now, let's consider the Gravestone Doji:

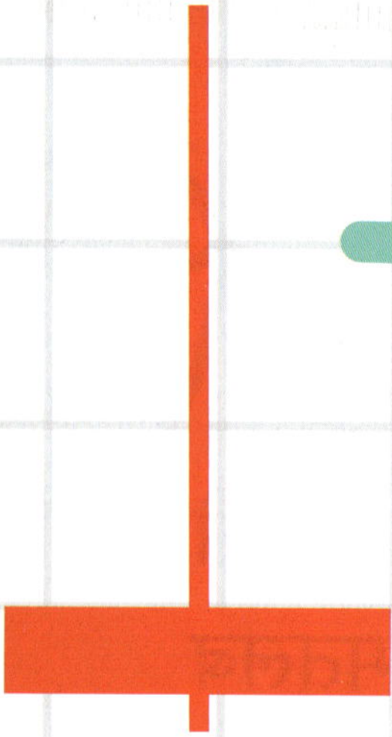

GRAVESTONE DOJI

- Assume the same stock XYZ is trading at ₹70.
- A Gravestone Doji forms, with the opening price at ₹70, the high at ₹100 and the closing price at ₹65.

For the Gravestone Doji:

- Entry Price: Since the Gravestone Doji indicates potential bearish reversal, a trader might consider entering a sell trade slightly below the low of the Gravestone Doji. So, let's say the entry price is set at ₹65.
- Stop Loss: To manage risk, a stop-loss order can be placed above the high of the Gravestone Doji. So, let's set the stop-loss price at ₹100.

DRAGONFLY DOJI

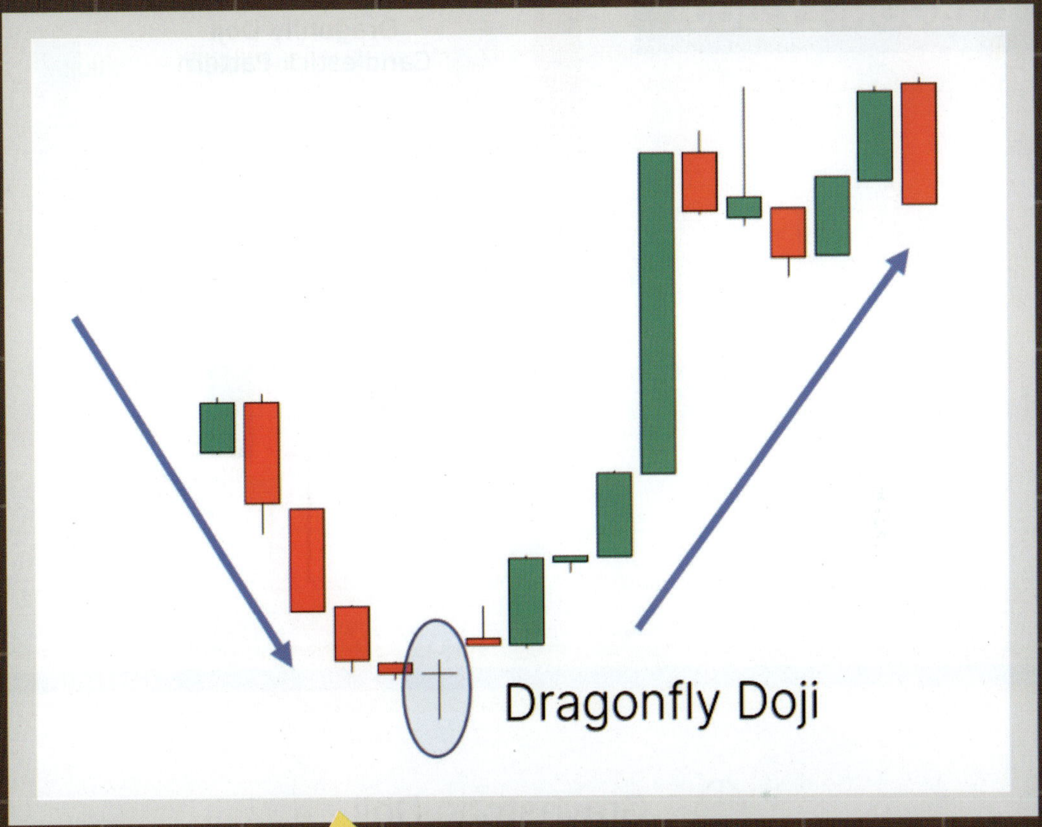

DID YOU KNOW?

The dragonfly doji candlestick pattern appears when the open, close, and high prices are all at the same level, with a long lower shadow. This pattern signals potential bullish reversal, especially after a downtrend, as it shows that buyers have regained control and pushed prices back up. When confirmed by a subsequent bullish candle, it can indicate a strong shift in market sentiment!

SPOTTING ON THE CHART

DRAGONFLY DOJI

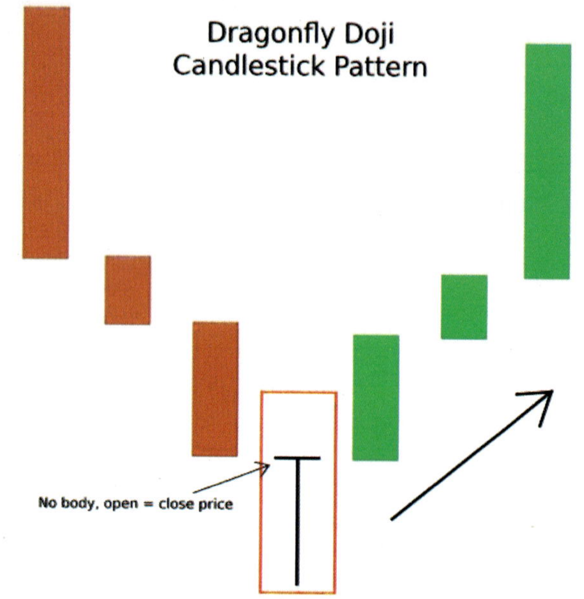

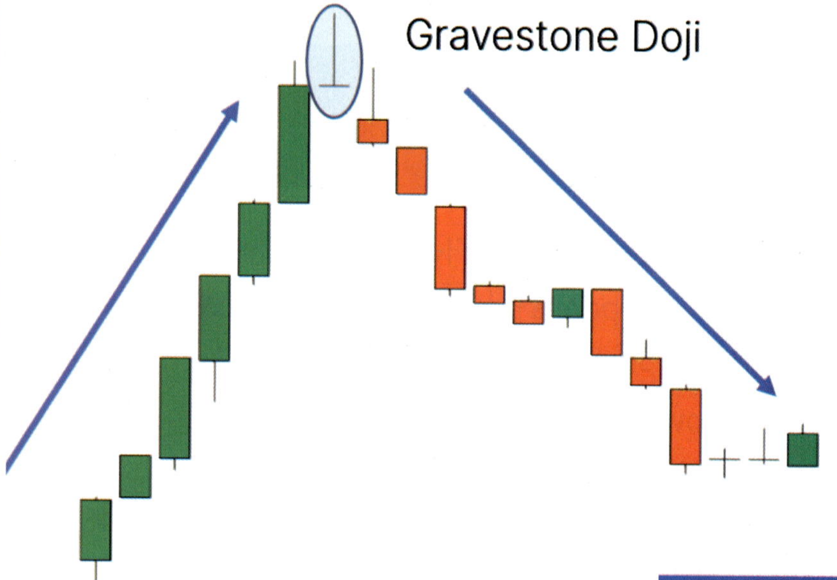

GRAVESTONE DOJI

INDIA'S ONLY 24X7 TRADING EXCHANGE:

NSE IFSC, the International Financial Services Centre of the NSE, launched in Gujarat's GIFT City, operates 24/7 for international investors. It was India's attempt to bring in global liquidity and make Indian equities accessible around the clock.

ACTIVITY TIME

On March 20 2024 a Dragonfly Doji Candlestick Pattern is formed on a Daily Time Frame on the Sunteck Realty Chart. Tell me what was the context of the market ?

- Share was in Uptrend
- Share was in Downtrend
- Share was in Downtrend and pattern is formed near support

On September 05, 2024, a Gravestone Doji is Formed on GNFC(stock name). Tell the Time frame of the Chart.

- 1 hour
- Daily
- Weekly
- Monthly

BULLISH

& BEARISH SPINNING TOP

PATTERN 4

SPINNING TOP CANDLESTICK

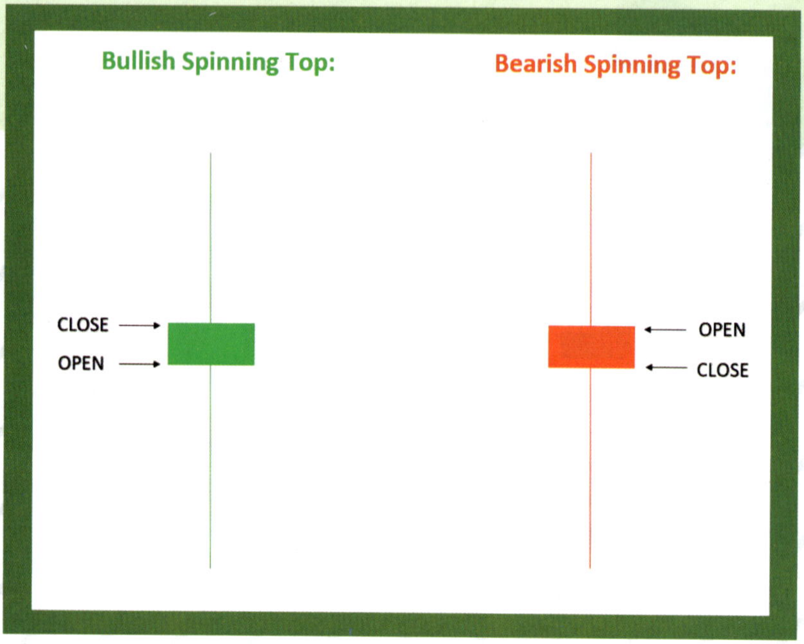

Spinning top candlestick pattern तब बनता है जब opening और closing prices एक दूसरे के बहुत करीब होते हैं, और atleast 2 times longer upper and lower wicks होती हैं। ये market में uncertainty को दिखाता है।

ANALYSIS:

1. Market Sentiment: Spinning top suggest करता है कि buyers और sellers के बीच एक तरह का tussle चल रहा है।
2. Price Action: Lambi upper और lower wicks show करते हैं कि trading period में price में significant movement हुआ है ऊपर-नीचे, लेकिन price end में opening level के करीब close होता है। This shows ki market में directional clear नहीं है and Market is uncertain.
3. Potential Reversal: Spinning top खुद में reversal को confirm नहीं करता, लेकिन अक्सर downtrend or uptrend के दौरान next candle के confirmation में हम लोग decide करते हैं कि reversal है या नहीं।

एक bullish spinning top candlestick pattern तब बनता है जब opening और closing prices एक दूसरे के बहुत करीब होते हैं, और atleast 2 times longer upper and lower wicks होती हैं। ये market में uncertainty को दिखाता है, और थोड़ा सा bullish bias भी होता है।

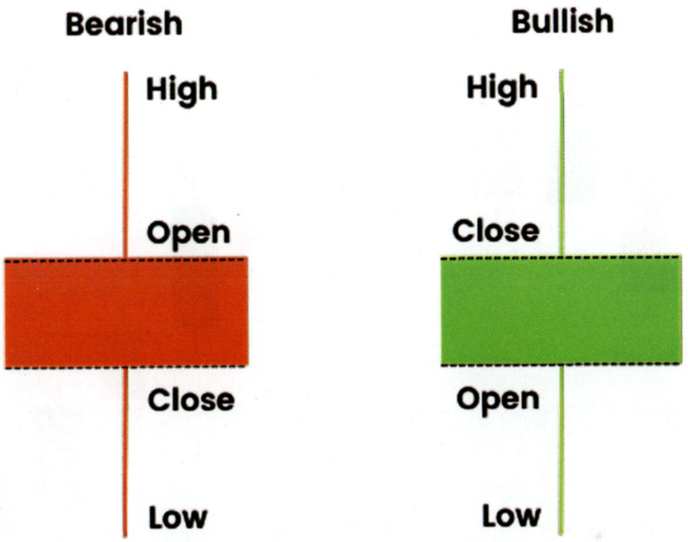

ANALYSIS:

1. Market Sentiment: Bullish spinning top suggest करता है कि buyers और sellers के बीच एक तरह का tussle चल रहा है, लेकिन buyers थोड़ा सा dominant होते हैं।
2. Price Action: Lambi upper और lower wicks show करते हैं कि trading period में price में significant movement हुआ है ऊपर-नीचे, लेकिन price end में opening level के करीब close होता है।
3. Potential Reversal: Bullish spinning top खुद में reversal को confirm नहीं करता, लेकिन ये अक्सर downtrends के दौरान होता है और अगला candle bullish है तो ये एक possible uptrend की indication दे सकता है।

SPOTTING ON CHART

BEARISH SPINNING TOP CANDLESTICK PATTERN

Bearish Spinning Top:

एक bearish spinning top candlestick pattern तब बनता है जब opening और closing prices एक doosre के बहुत करीब होते हैं, और लंबी upper और lower wicks होती हैं। ये market में uncertainty को दिखाता है, लेकिन थोड़ा सा bearish biased होता है।

Analysis:

1. Market Sentiment: Bearish spinning top suggest करता है कि buyers और sellers ke beech एक tarah ka tussle chal raha hai, लेकिन sellers thoda sa dominant hote hain.
2. Price Action: Lambi upper और lower wicks ke saath price में significant movement hoti hai upar neeche, लेकिन price end में opening level ke kareeb close होता है।
3. Potential Reversal: Bearish spinning top khud में reversal को confirm नहीं करता, लेकिन ये अकसर uptrends के दौरान होता है और अगला candle bearish है तो ये एक possible downtrend की indication दे सकता है।

SPOTTING ON CHART

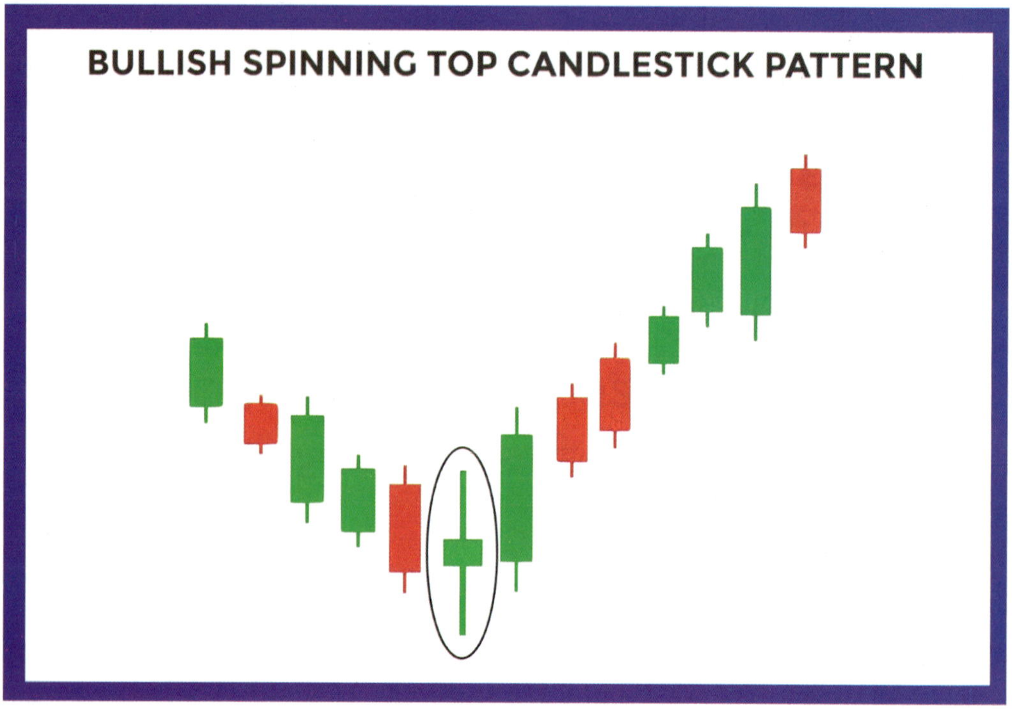

Dono cases में, traders आगे के candles से confirmation का wait करते हैं जो spinning top pattern द्वारा suggest की गई reversal को validate करते हैं। ये confirmation strong bullish या bearish candlestick pattern के रूप में आती है जो expected reversal direction के साथ align होती है। साथ ही, traders दूसरे technical indicators और market context को भी consider करते हैं informed trading decisions के लिए। Note: Spinning tops की wicks/shadows जितनी longer होती है, pattern उतना ही strong signal indicate करता है. Wick length ∝ Strength of Trend signal

UNUSUAL SUSPENSION:

In 2013, an error during trading caused a steep 16% fall in the NSE's Nifty index within just 10 minutes. This led to a temporary suspension, making it one of the rare instances of trading suspension due to a technical glitch.

ACTIVITY TIME

On September 05, 2024 A spinning Top candlestick pattern is formed ,On Lalpath (stock name) on Hourly Time frame. Identify the next candle ?

- Bearish Candle
- Bullish Candle
- Hammer
- Doji

On December 10 2018, a bullish spinning top candlestick pattern was formed on Canfinhome(stock name) on a Daily Time Frame. What was the overall trend of the stock?

- Downtrend
- Uptrend
- Sideway

BULLISH & BEARISH MARUZOBU

PATTERN 5

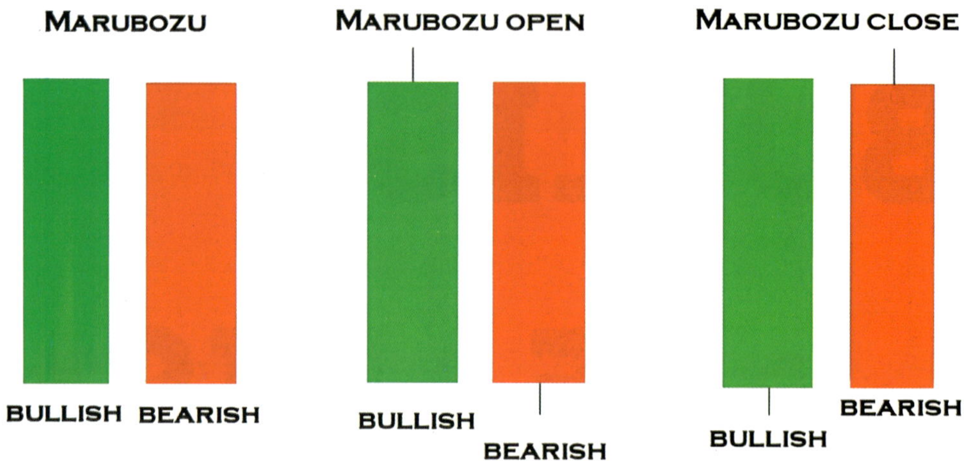

Marubozu candlestick patterns को समझना काफी important है। "Marubozu" शब्द Japanese है , इसका meaning है कि ये candlesticks के दोनों किनारों पर छोटी-छोटी shadow(wicks) होती है या बिल्कुल भी shadows नहीं होती। ये pattern दिखाता है कि trading session में एकदम ज़ोरदार buying या selling का दबाव है। This is a very strong trading pattern तो इसको trends confirm करने के लिए भी use किया जाता है।

STRUCTURE OF THE MARUBOZU CANDLESTICK:

BODY

The body of a Marubozu is long and represents the price range between the opening and closing prices of the session. If it's a bullish Marubozu, the closing price is higher than the opening price, and the body is typically white or green. Conversely, if it's a bearish Marubozu, the closing price is lower than the opening price, and the body is usually black or red.

WICKS/SHADOWS

A Marubozu has little to no wicks or shadows. If any wicks or shadows are present, they are very short relative to the length of the body. This indicates that there was minimal price movement beyond the opening or closing price during the session.

OPENING AND CLOSING PRICES

The opening price is either the highest or lowest price of the session, depending on whether it's a bullish or bearish Marubozu. Similarly, the closing price is either the highest or lowest price of the session, opposite to the opening price.

LENGTH

The length of the body of a Marubozu is significant. A longer body indicates a more decisive move, while a shorter body may suggest less conviction in the market move.

BULLISH MARUBOZU:

Bullish Marubozu में long body होती है और उसके दोनों ends पर कोई shadows नहीं होती। ये आमतौर पर downtrend दिखता है।

Significance: ऊपर और नीचे की shadows के absence का मतलब है कि पूरे trading session में bull (खरीदने वाले/buyers) ने dominance रखी है, जो कि strong buying signals को दर्शाता है। ये bearish sentiment से bullish sentiment में एक reversal indicate करता है।

BEARISH MARUBOZU:

Bearish Marubozu में भी long body होती है और उसके दोनों ends पर कोई shadows नहीं होती। ये आमतौर पर uptrend दिखता है।

Significance: Shadows के absence या बिल्कुल negligible होने का मतलब है कि पूरे trading session में bear (बेचने वाले/sellers) ने dominance रखी थी, जो कि strong selling का signal देता है। ये bullish sentiment से bearish sentiment में एक strong reversal को indicate करता है।

HOW TO SPOT MARUBOZU ON A CHART?

Bullish Marubozu: Plot a long green candlestick with minimal or no upper and lower wicks, indicating strong buying pressure, typically appearing in a downtrend.

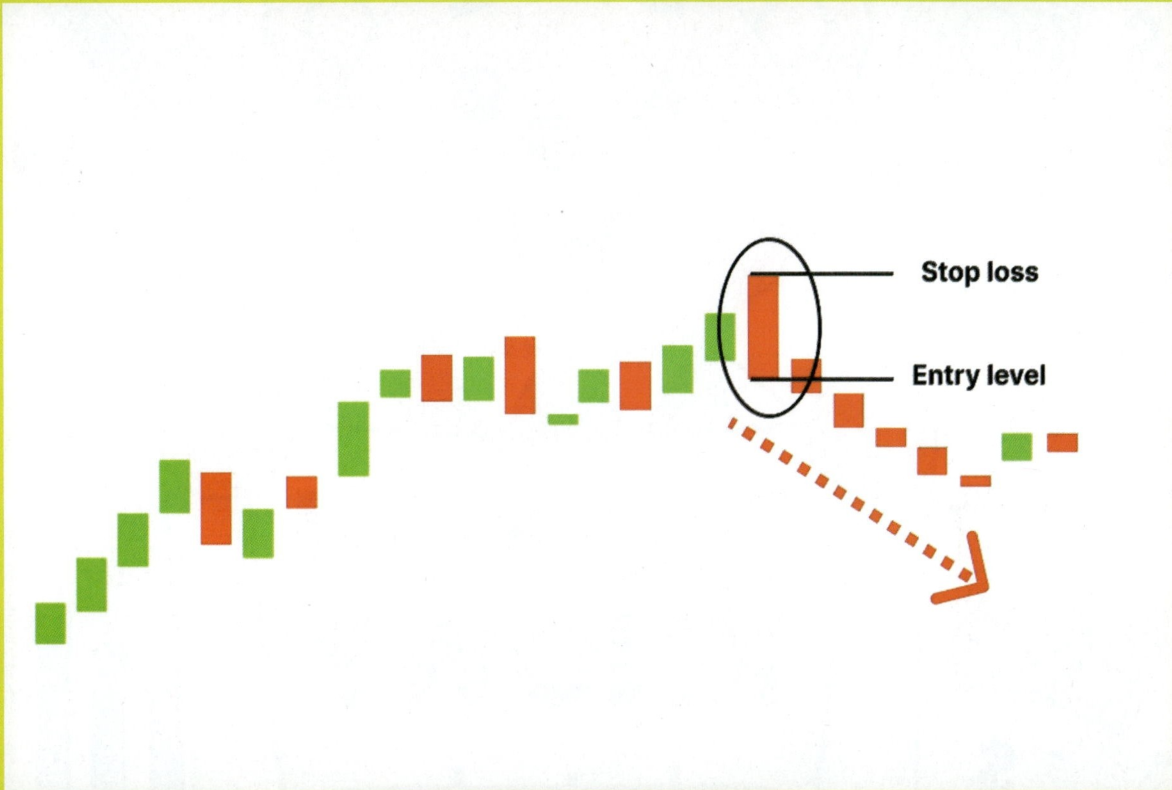
Stop loss
Entry level

NIFTY BEEHIVE THEORY:

Analysts noticed that Nifty oscillates in ranges, behaving like a beehive with set thresholds for movement. When the index hits certain support or resistance levels, it tends to consolidate there, an unusual and unique pattern for Indian indices.

ACTIVITY TIME

See GEPIl (stock name) From date (01-12-2013 to 30-12-2013) tell how many Bearish Marubozu candle are their on Weekly Time Frame ?

- 4
- 3
- 0
- 2

See GEPIL weekly chart on 13 Nov 2023 ?

Tell the pattern name ?

- Bearish harami
- Bullish harami
- Tweezer top
- Bullish marubozu

NOTES

3.

Two Candlesticks patterns

In the previous chapter we talked about single candlestick patterns that are formed by one candlestick on the chart. In the current chapter we are going to talk about candlestick patterns formed by two candlesticks on the trading chart.

BULLISH & BEARISH FLYING KICKER

PATTERN 1

FLYING KICKERS

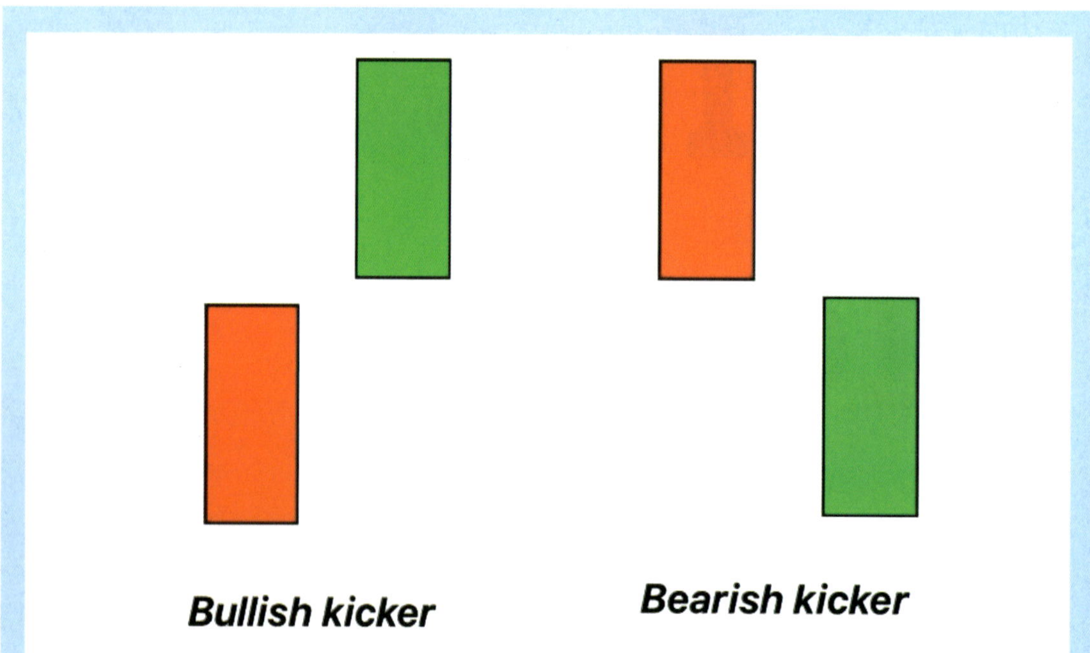

Candlestick patterns market analysis में काफी important role play करते हैं। इसमें दो candlesticks एक नया pattern बनाते हैं जो traders को market के mood को समझने में मदद करता है। इसका नाम "Flying Kicker" इसलिए है क्योंकि ये patterns market में movement को indicate करते हैं, जैसे एक Japanese fighter तेज़ी से ऊपर या नीचे kick करता है।

BULLISH FLYING KICKER

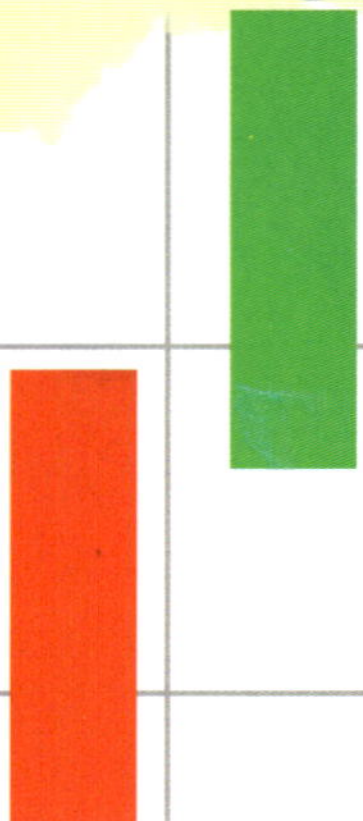

THESE ARE AS FOLLOWS

Market Sentiment: Bullish Flying Kicker का simple मतलब है कि buyers और sellers के बीच में strong buying sentiment है, जिससे market में तेज़ी का sentiment है। ये pattern downtrend के दौरान दिखता है और एक possible uptrend की starting को दर्शाता है।

Price Action: इस pattern में पहली candle bearish होती है, मतलब sellers कोशिश करते हैं price को नीचे लाने की लेकिन दूसरी ही candle में buyers dominant हो जाते हैं and candle bullish हो जाता है और पहले से बड़े gap up पे open होती है। ये एक bullish momentum को दर्शाता है।

Potential Reversal: Bullish Flying Kicker को देखकर traders को लगता है कि अब market का trend change होने वाला है, लेकिन confirmation के लिए अगले candles का wait किया जाता है। अगर अगला candle भी bullish है तो यह uptrend की shuruaat का indication है।

BEARISH FLYING KICKER

THESE ARE AS FOLLOWS:

Market Sentiment: Bearish Flying Kicker का matlab है कि sellers ने market में dominance दिखा रखी है और selling pressure strong है। ये pattern uptrend के दौरान दिखता है और एक possible downtrend की starting को दर्शाता है।

Potential Reversal: Bearish Flying Kicker देखकर traders को lagta है कि अब market का trend change होने वाला है, लेकिन confirmation के लिए agle candles का wait किया जाता है। अगर अगला candle भी bearish है तो यह downtrend की starting का indication है।

Price Action: इस pattern में पहला candle bullish होता है, लेकिन दूसरा candle bearish होता है और पहले से बड़े gap down पे open होता है। ये एक bearish momentum को दर्शाता है।

Dono cases में traders को aage के candles की confirmation का इंतज़ार होता है जो pattern द्वारा suggest की गई reversal को validate करते हैं। ये confirmation strong bullish या bearish candlestick pattern के form में आती है जो expected reversal direction के saath align होती है। साथ ही, traders दूसरे technical indicators और market context को भी consider करते हैं to take informed trading decisions.

SPOTTING A FLYING KICKER ON A CHART USING MARUBOZU SINGLE CANDLESTICKS

To spot a flying kicker pattern on a chart using single candlesticks, particularly Marubozu candlesticks, you need to observe the formation of two consecutive Marubozu candles that indicate a potential trend reversal. Here's how you can identify a bullish and bearish flying kicker using Marubozu candlesticks.

BULLISH FLYING KICKER	BEARISH FLYING KICKER
Look for a downtrend where the market has been consistently moving lower.	Look for an uptrend where the market has been consistently moving higher.
Identify a bearish Marubozu candlestick, which indicates strong selling pressure. This candle should be followed by:	Identify a bullish Marubozu candlestick, which indicates strong buying pressure. This candle should be followed by:
A bullish Marubozu candlestick with a significant gap up from the previous close, indicating a strong opening by buyers. This candlestick closing higher than the previous candle's close confirms bullish momentum	A bearish Marubozu candlestick with a significant gap down from the previous close, indicating a strong opening by sellers. This candlestick closing lower than the previous candle's close confirms bearish momentum.

" By observing these Marubozu candlestick formations, traders can spot potential flying kicker patterns indicating trend reversals. However, it's essential to wait for confirmation from subsequent price action to validate the reversal signal. "

EXAMPLES

EXAMPLE 1

1. Imagine we're looking at a stock that's been consistently falling in price

EXAMPLES 2

2. On Day 1, you see a bearish Marubozu candlestick. The stock opens at ₹100 and closes at ₹80. In this case open= high and close= low. This shows strong selling pressure.

EXAMPLE 3

3. On Day 2, you notice a bullish Marubozu candlestick with a big gap up from the previous day's close. It opens at ₹110,reaches a high and closes at ₹130. This candlestick closing higher than the previous day's close signals bullish momentum and suggests a possible bullish reversal.

WHEN TO ENTER THE TRADE?

Traders might consider entering a buying trade after the close of Day 2, once the bullish momentum is confirmed. Entering the trade at the opening price of Day 3 or slightly above it could be a strategic entry point.

WHERE TO PLACE THE STOP-LOSS:

A prudent place to set the stop-loss could be below the low of the bullish Marubozu candlestick formed on Day 2.

BULLISH FLYING KICKER

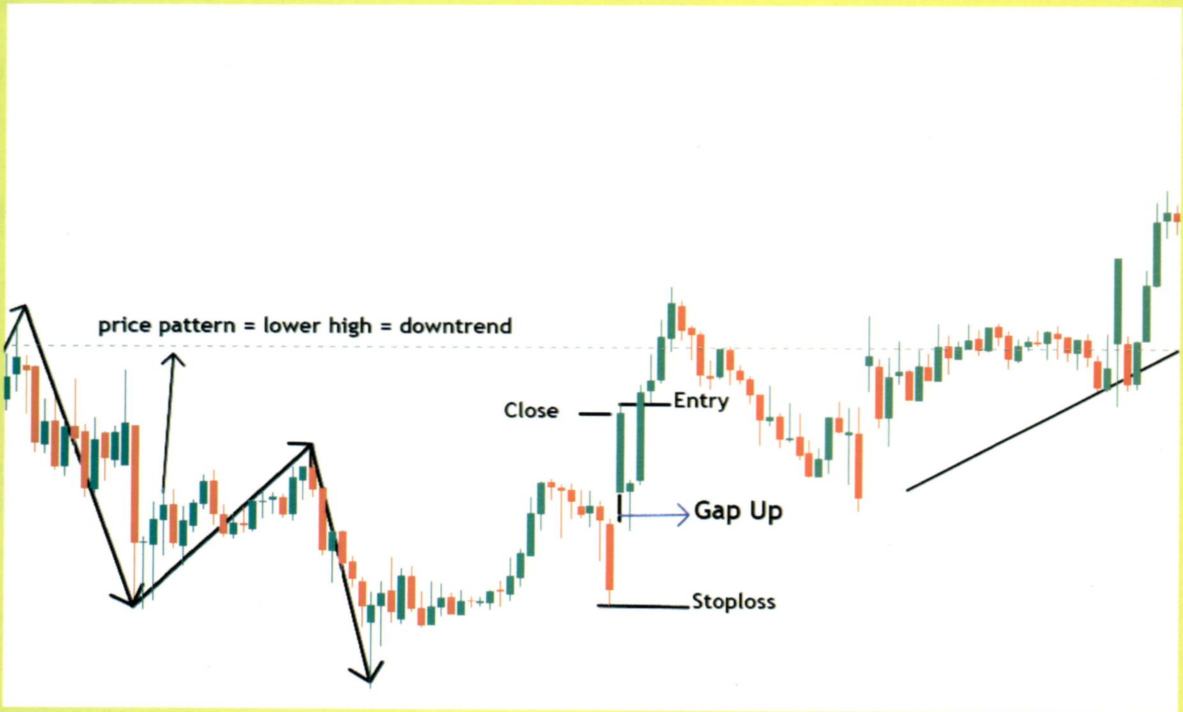

DID YOU KNOW?

It is a strong reversal signal in technical analysis, where after a clear downtrend, a large bearish candle is followed by a gap up and a significant bullish candle. The gap between the two candles, with no overlap, is a key feature that shows a sudden shift in market sentiment from bearish to bullish. This pattern reflects a decisive control by buyers, often interpreted as an entry signal for a long position, expecting the uptrend to continue. The bullish flying kicker is considered one of the most reliable indicators of a sharp reversal.

BEARISH FLYING KICKER:

STEP 1

1. Now let's consider a stock that's been on an upward trend.

STEP 2

2. On Day 1, you see a bullish Marubozu candlestick. The stock opens at ₹100, reaches a high and closes at ₹130. This indicates strong buying pressure.

STEP 3

3. On Day 2, you observe a bearish Marubozu candlestick with a significant gap down from the previous day's close. It opens at ₹90, hits a high and low of ₹70, and closes at ₹70. This candlestick closing lower than the previous day's close confirms bearish momentum and hints at a possible bearish reversal.

WHEN TO ENTER THE TRADE:

- Traders may contemplate entering a selling trade after the close of Day 2, once the bearish momentum is confirmed. Entering the trade at the opening price of Day 3 or slightly below it could be a strategic entry point. In this case the Day 3 Candle does not provide confirmation as it doesn't close below the low of second candle, so we take confirmation from the 4th Day candlestick and use it's closing price as entry point.

WHERE TO PLACE THE STOP-LOSS

- A strategic location to set the stop-loss could be above the high of the bearish Marubozu candlestick formed on Day 2.

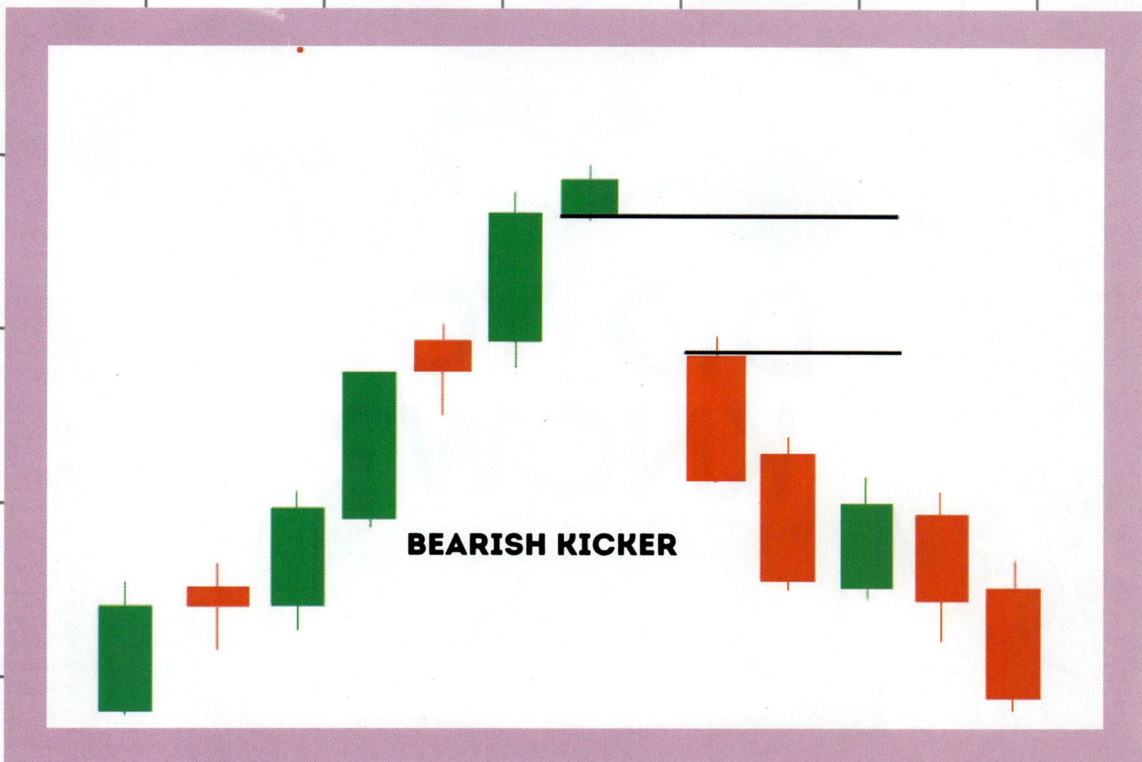

Note: It might not always be the case की Kicker pattern की candlestick Marubozu form में ही बने, हो सकता है की थोड़ी सी shadows भी देखने को मिले। अगर perfect Marubozu candlesticks से ये pattern बनता है तो it is a strong signal otherwise signal की intensity thodi सी कम मानी जा सकती है।

THE POWER OF RETAIL INVESTORS:

The retail investor base in India has grown dramatically in recent years, reaching over 12 crore demat accounts by 2023. The rise is largely due to digital trading platforms and increased financial literacy efforts.

ACTIVITY TIME

What was the key Feature of Bullish Flying kicker ?

- It is formed in uptrend
- It is 1 candle stick pattern
- It has gap between 2 candle with no overlap .

ACTIVITY TIME

When to enter trade after bearish flying kicker candlestick pattern is formed ?

- After opening
- After closing of Day 2
- Do not enter.

ACTIVITY TIME

What was the key Feature of Bullish Flying kicker ?

- It is formed in uptrend
- It is 1 candle stick pattern
- It has gap between 2 candle with no overlap .

ACTIVITY TIME

When to enter trade after bearish flying kicker candlestick pattern is formed ?

- After opening
- After closing of Day 2
- Do not enter.

BULLISH & BEARISH ENGULFING

PATTERN 2

ENGULFING CANDLESTICK PATTERNS

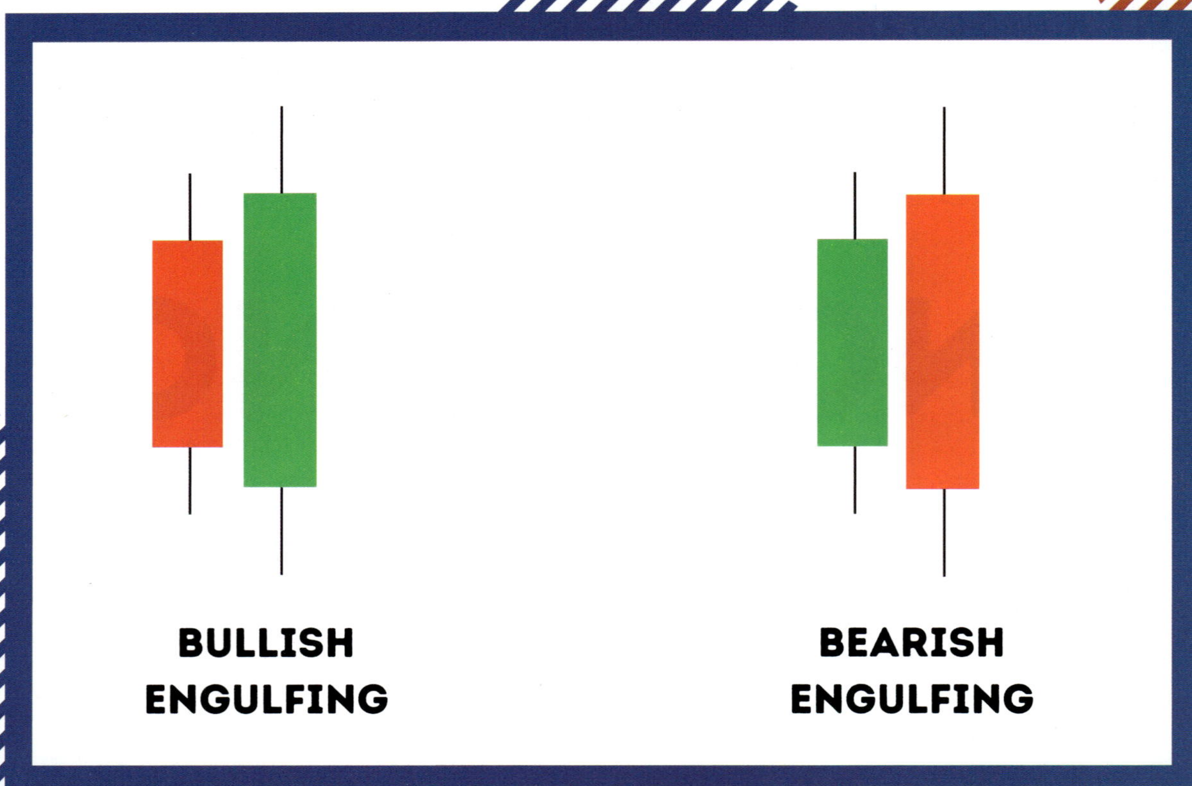

Engulfing candlestick patterns दो candlesticks से बनते हैं. "Engulfing" का मतलब है कि एक candlestick दूसरे को पूरी तरह से engulf कर लेता है, जैसे कि एक बड़ी मछली छोटे मछली को निगल लेती है।

PSYCHOLOGY OF ENGULFING PATTERN

The engulfing pattern in market psychology signals a potential reversal. In a bullish engulfing pattern, sellers dominate early but are overpowered by buyers, showing a shift in momentum. Conversely, a bearish engulfing pattern sees buyers initially in control, but sellers take over, signaling potential downside. Traders interpret this as a clear change in sentiment—either optimism (bullish) or pessimism (bearish). The larger body of the engulfing candle compared to the previous one reflects the stronger conviction. Engulfing patterns are often viewed as more reliable when they appear at significant support or resistance levels.

BULLISH ENGULFING:

- जब एक छोटा bearish candlestick(red) एक bade bullish candlestick(green) से पूरी तरह से cover हो जाता है, तो ये एक bullish engulfing pattern बनाता है। ये pattern downtrend को रोकने और possible uptrend की shuruaat का indication देता है।

STRUCTURE:

- **First Candlestick:** एक छोटा bearish (red) candle जो current downtrend को दिखाता है।

- **Second Candlestick:** एक बड़ा bullish (green) candle जो पहले candlestick के body को completely engulf करता है, indicating a strong reversal signal.

MARKET PSYCHOLOGY

यह pattern market sentiment में एक significant shift को indicate करता है। पहला bearish candlestick sellers के control को दिखाता है। Dusra bullish candlestick strong buying pressure को दिखाता है जो previous bearish candle को engulf करता है, indicating a potential bullish reversal.

BEARISH ENGULFING:

• जब एक छोटा bullish candlestick एक bade bearish candlestick से पूरी तरह से cover हो जाता है, तो ये एक bearish engulfing pattern बनाता है। ये pattern uptrend को रोकने और possible downtrend की शुरुआत का indication देता है।

STRUCTURE:

• **First Candlestick:** एक छोटा bullish (green) candle जो current uptrend को दिखाता है।

• **Second Candlestick:** एक बड़ा bearish (red) candle जो पहले candlestick के body को completely engulf करता है, indicating a strong reversal signal.

MARKET PSYCHOLOGY

यह pattern market sentiment में एक significant shift को indicate करता है। पहला bullish candlestick buyers के control को दिखाता है। दूसरा bearish candlestick strong selling pressure को दिखाता है जो previous bullish candle को engulf करता है, indicating a potential bearish reversal

BULLISH ENGULFING: EXAMPLES

1. **Day 1**: A small bearish candlestick forms with the open at ₹50, the high and low at ₹52 and ₹48, and the close at ₹48.

2. **Day 2:** A large bullish candlestick forms and completely engulfs the body of the bearish candlestick from Day 1. The open is ₹48, the high and low are ₹55 and ₹45, and the close is ₹55.

When to Enter the Buying Trade & Where to Place Stop Loss?

- **Entry:** Traders might consider entering a buying trade after the close of Day 2, once the bullish reversal is confirmed. Entering the trade at the opening price of Day 3 or slightly above it could be a strategic entry point.

- **Stop Loss:** A prudent place to set the stop-loss could be below the low of the bullish engulfing candlestick formed on Day 2. Setting the stop-loss at ₹45 or slightly below it could help mitigate risk in case the reversal doesn't materialize, and the price turns bearish again.

SPOTTING THE BULLISH ENGULFING PATTERN ON THE CHART:

- To spot the bullish engulfing pattern on the chart, look for a small bearish candlestick followed by a larger bullish candlestick that completely engulfs the body of the bearish candlestick. This indicates a potential bullish reversal.

BEARISH ENGULFING:

- **Day 1**: A small bullish candlestick forms with the open at ₹60, the high and low at ₹55 and ₹63, and the close at ₹62.

- **Day 2**: A large bearish candlestick forms and completely engulfs the body of the bullish candlestick from Day 1. The open is ₹62, the high and low are ₹55 and ₹63, and the close is ₹55.

When to Enter the Selling Trade and Where to Place Stop Loss?

- Entry: Traders may contemplate entering a selling trade after the close of Day 2, once the bearish reversal is confirmed. Entering the trade at the opening price of Day 3 or slightly below it could be a strategic entry point.

- Stop Loss: A strategic location to set the stop-loss could be above the high of the bearish engulfing candlestick formed on Day 2. Setting the stop-loss at ₹63 or slightly above it could help manage risk in case the anticipated reversal doesn't occur, and the price continues to rise.

SPOTTING THE BEARISH ENGULFING PATTERN ON THE CHART:

To spot the bearish engulfing pattern on the chart, look for a small bullish candlestick followed by a larger bearish candlestick that completely engulfs the body of the bullish candlestick. This indicates a potential bearish reversal.

FII-DOMINATED MARKET:

Foreign Institutional Investors (FIIs) have had a significant impact on market sentiment. On days with high FII inflows, markets tend to rise, while outflows tend to bring markets down, showing the influence of global capital in Indian markets.

ACTIVITY TIME

On 23 aug 2018 bearish engulfing pattern formed on Daily Time Frame On Exide Industries Chart. Tell prior trend of the market ?

- Uptrend
- Downtrend
- Sideway

What is psychology of bullish engulfing pattern choose the correct answer?

- Shift in Momentum
- Shift in Momentum from bearish to bullish
- It shows the beginning of the downtrend

BULLISH & BEARISH HARAMI

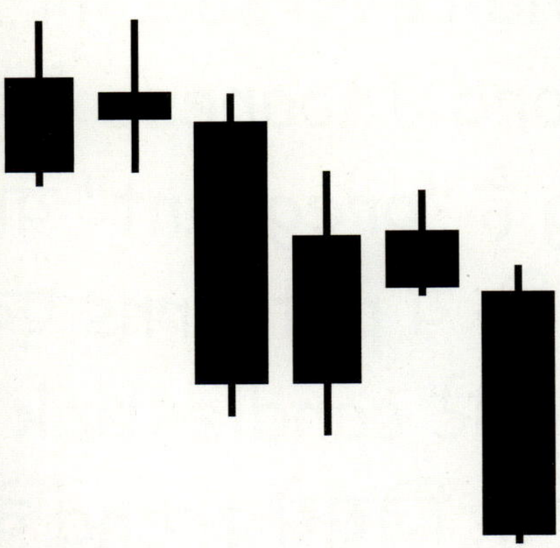

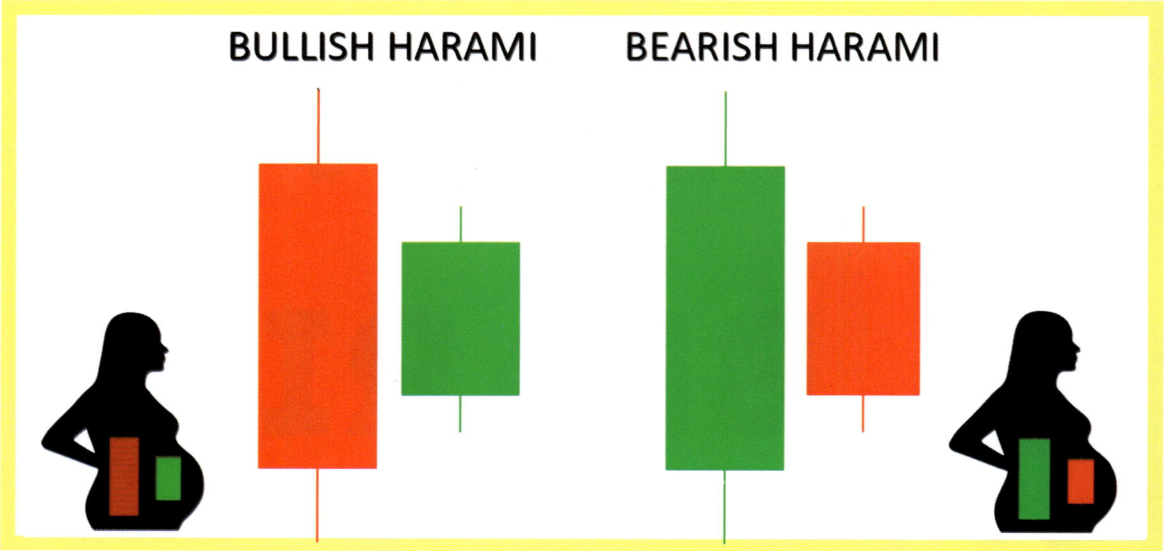

Harami candlestick pattern दो candlesticks से बनते हैं और market के trend reversals को indicate करते हैं। "Harami" word Japanese है और इसका Japanese में meaning है "pregnant" या "with child", इसका मतलब है कि ये patterns एक bade candlestick के अंदर एक छोटे candlestick को "pregnant" या "carry" करते हैं, जिससे trend के reversal का indication मिलता है।

BULLISH AND BEARISH HARAMI

BULLISH HARAMI

VS

- जब एक bada bearish candlestick, जो एक downtrend के दौरान दिखता है,उसके बाद एक छोटा bullish candlestick आ जाए जो पहले के candlestick के बिल्कुल अंदर fit होता है, तो ये एक bullish harami pattern बनाता है। ये pattern downtrend को रोकने और possible uptrend की शुरुआत का indication देता है।

BEARISH HARAMI

- जब एक बड़ा bullish candlestick, जो एक uptrend के दौरान दिखता है, उसके बाद एक छोटा bearish candlestick आ जाए जो पहले के candlestick के बिल्कुल अंदर fit होता है, तो ये एक bearish harami pattern बनाता है। ये pattern uptrend को rokne और possible downtrend की शुरुआत का indication देता है।

Note: Doosri candlestick, पहली candlestick के अंदर fit होनी चाहिए। अगर उसकी body बाहर निकल जाती है तो वो Harami pattern नहीं बनेगा।

EXAMPLE:

BULLISH HARAMI:

1. **Day 1:** A bearish candlestick forms with the open at ₹50, the high and low at ₹52 and ₹48, and the close at ₹48.

2. **Day 2:** A smaller bullish candlestick forms within the body of the bearish candlestick, with a gap up open at ₹49, the high and low at ₹50.5 and ₹48.5, and the close at ₹50.

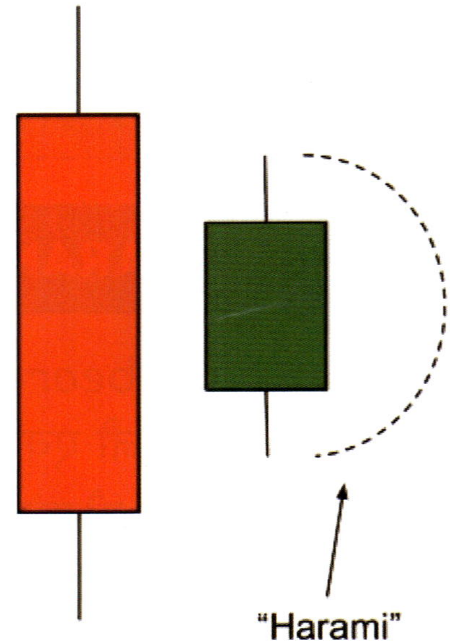

WHEN TO ENTER THE BUYING TRADE & WHERE TO PLACE STOP LOSS:

- **Entry:** Traders might consider entering a buying trade after the close of Day 2, once the bullish reversal is confirmed. Entering the trade at the opening price of Day 3 or slightly above it could be a strategic entry point.
- **Stop Loss:** A prudent place to set the stop-loss could be below the low of the bullish candlestick formed on Day 2. Setting the stop-loss at ₹48 or slightly below it could help mitigate risk in case the reversal doesn't materialize, and the price turns bearish again.

SPOTTING THE BULLISH HARAMI PATTERN ON THE CHART:

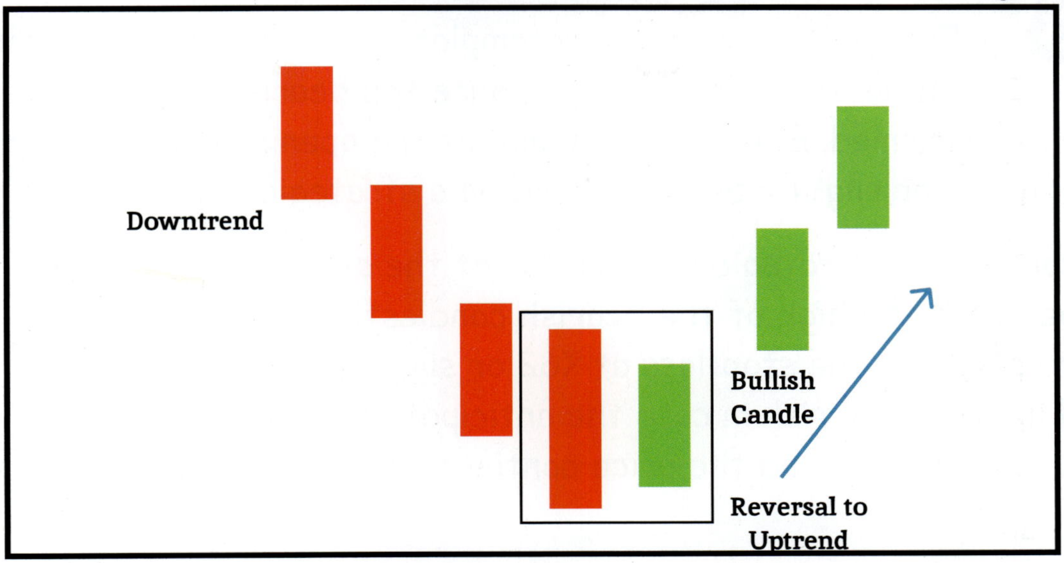

- To spot the bullish harami pattern on the chart, look for a larger bearish candlestick followed by a smaller bullish candlestick that fits entirely within the body of the bearish candlestick. This indicates a potential bullish reversal.

EXAMPLE:

BEARISH HARAMI:

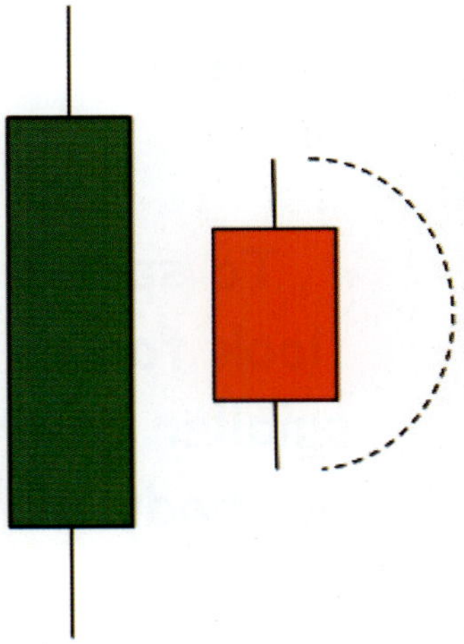

1. Day 1: A bullish candlestick forms with the open at ₹60, the high and low at ₹65 and₹57, and the close at ₹62.
2. Day 2: A smaller bearish candlestick forms within the body of the bullish candlestick, with the gap down open at ₹61, the high and low at ₹62 and₹68, and the close at ₹59.

WHEN TO ENTER THE BUYING TRADE AND WHERE TO PLACE STOP LOSS

- **Entry:** Traders may contemplate entering a selling trade after the close of Day 2, once the bearish reversal is confirmed. Entering the trade at the opening price of Day 3 or slightly below it could be a strategic entry point.

- **Stop Loss**: A strategic location to set the stop-loss could be above the high of the bearish candlestick formed on Day 2. Setting the stop-loss at ₹62 or slightly above it could help manage risk in case the anticipated reversal doesn't occur, and the price continues to rise.

SPOTTING THE BEARISH HARAMI PATTERN ON THE CHART:

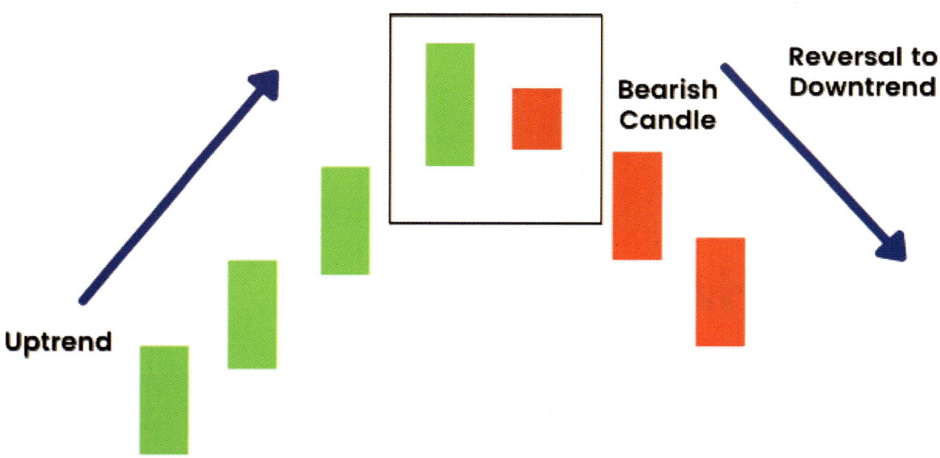

- To spot the bearish harami pattern on the chart, look for a larger bullish candlestick followed by a smaller bearish candlestick that fits entirely within the body of the bullish candlestick. This indicates a potential bearish reversal.

STOCK WITH THE HIGHEST NOMINAL PRICE:

MRF shares are known for having the highest nominal price per share in the Indian market, often trading over ₹1 lakh per share. This high price is partly due to the company's policy of not splitting its shares.

ACTIVITY TIME

When a Bullish Harami Pattern formed on the daily chart of Lauruslabs (stock name) on 20th june 2022, what was the subsequent price movement? Did it confirm the anticipated uptrend ?

- Yes
- No

PIERCING LINE & DARK CLOUD COVER

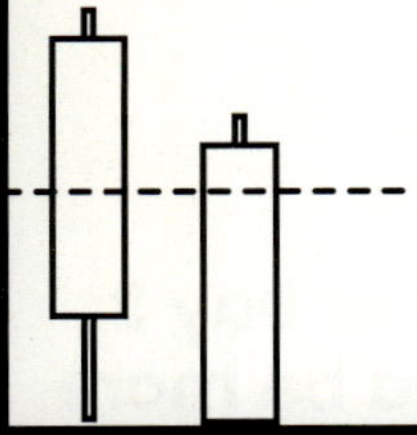

PATTERN 4

Piercing Pattern

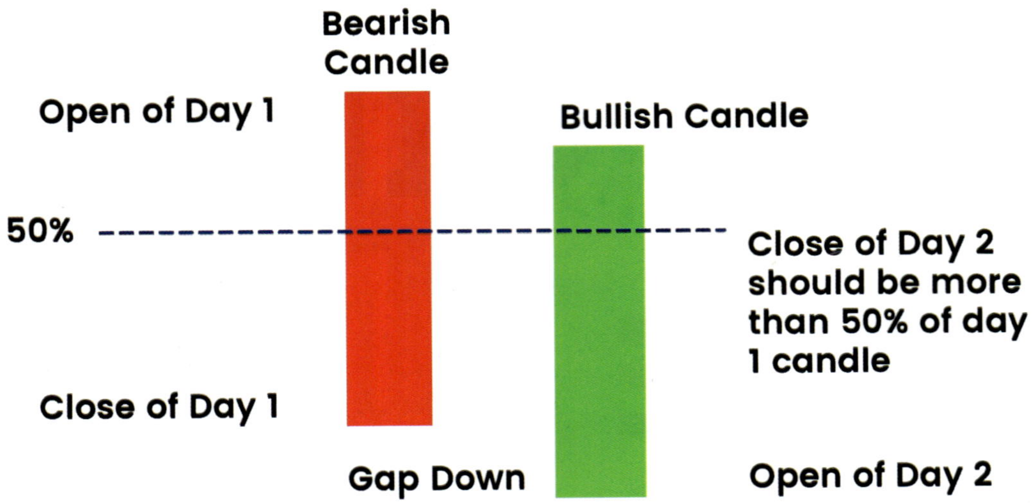

Dark Cloud Cover

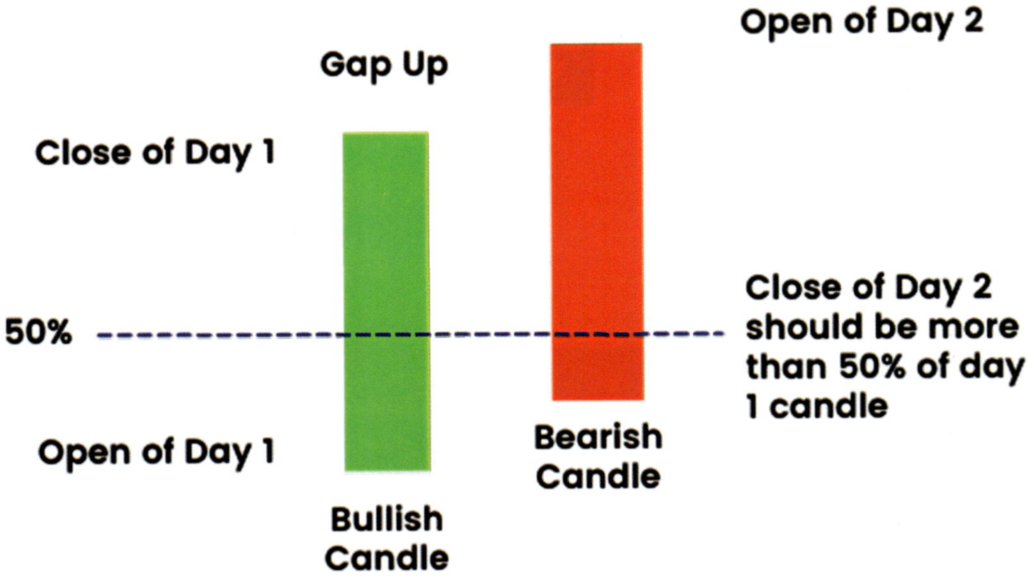

PIERCING LINE

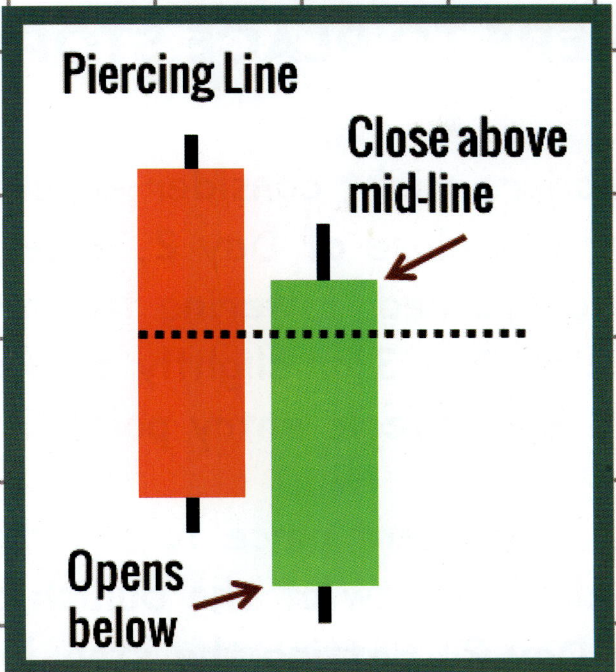

OVERVIEW:

Piercing Line candlestick pattern एक bullish reversal signal है जो downtrend के बाद appear होता है। ये pattern market के sentiment के reversal को indicate करता है और trend के ऊपर जाने का indication देता है।

STRUCTURE:

First Candlestick: एक लंबा bearish (red) candle जो strong selling pressure को दिखाता है।

Second Candlestick: पहले candle के low के नीचे (gap-down) open होता है, लेकिन trading session के दौरान price ऊपर move करके पहले candle के body के midpoint के ऊपर close होता है।

When? TO ENTER THE BUYING TRADE AND WHERE TO PLACE STOP LOSS:

- Entry: Traders might consider entering a buying trade after the close of Day 2, once the bullish reversal is confirmed. Entering the trade at the opening price of Day 3 or slightly above it could be a strategic entry point.

- Stop Loss: A prudent place to set the stop-loss could be below the low of the bullish candlestick formed on Day 2. Setting the stop-loss slightly below it could help mitigate risk in case the reversal doesn't materialize and the price turns bearish again.

SPOTTING THE PIERCING LINE PATTERN ON THE CHART

To spot the Piercing Line pattern on the chart, look for a larger bearish candlestick followed by a smaller bullish candlestick that fits significantly into the body of the bearish candlestick and closes above its midpoint. This indicates a potential bullish reversal.

MARKET PSYCHOLOGY:

Piercing Line pattern में market sentiment का shift होता है। पहले, market lower open होता है bearish sentiment की वजह से, लेकिन bulls step in करके price को ऊपर push karte हैं और second candle को पहले bearish candle के midpoint के ऊपर close करते हैं। ये indicate करता है कि bulls strength gain कर रहे हैं और potential reversal हो सकता है।

EXAMPLES

- Day 1: Bearish candlestick forms with the open at ₹50, high at ₹52, low at ₹46, and close at ₹48.
- Day 2: A bullish Candlesticks Form with Gap down open and than close above 50% of the bearish candle. Open and low at ₹45 and ₹44 and high and close at ₹47 and ₹48 .

DARK CLOUD COVER

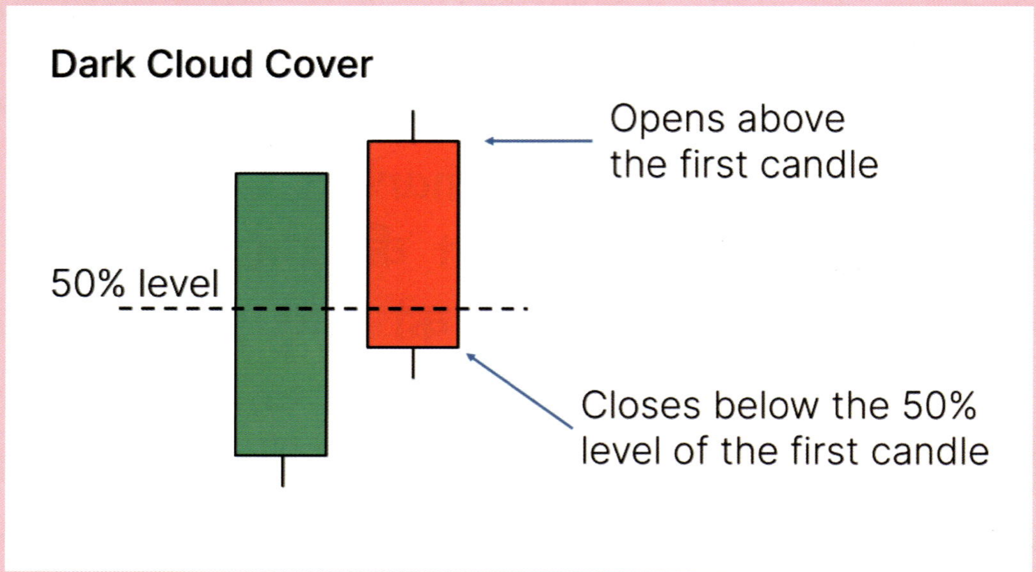

OVERVIEW:

Dark Cloud Cover candlestick pattern एक bearish reversal signal है जो uptrend के बाद appear होता है। ये pattern market के sentiment के reversal को indicate करता है और trend के नीचे जाने का indication देता है।

STRUCTURE:

1. **First Candlestick**: एक लंबा bullish (green) candle जो strong buying pressure को दिखाता है।
2. **Second Candlestick**: पहले candle के high के ऊपर (gap-up) open करता है, लेकिन trading session के दौरान price नीचे move करके पहले candle के body के midpoint के नीचे close होता है।

When? TO ENTER THE BUYING TRADE AND WHERE TO PLACE STOP LOSS:

- Entry: Traders might consider entering a selling trade after the close of Day 2, once the bullish reversal is confirmed. Entering the trade at the opening price of Day 3 or slightly below it could be a strategic entry point.

- Stop Loss: A prudent place to set the stop-loss could be above the high of the bullish candlestick formed on Day 2. Setting the stop-loss slightly above it could help mitigate risk in case the reversal doesn't materialize and the price turns bullish again.

SPOTTING THE PIERCING LINE PATTERN ON THE CHART

To spot the Dark Cloud Cover pattern on the chart, look for larger bullish candlesticks followed by a gap up open of second candle than second candle cut 50% of bullish candle and close below it.

MARKET PSYCHOLOGY:

The Dark Cloud Cover is a bearish reversal candlestick pattern that reflects a shift in market psychology from optimism to pessimism. It typically forms after a strong upward trend, signaling potential exhaustion of bullish momentum. The pattern starts with a long green candle, followed by a red candle that opens above the previous day's close but closes below the midpoint of the green candle. This suggests that sellers are gaining control, as buyers are unable to maintain the rally. Traders interpret this as a signal of a potential downturn, often leading to increased selling pressure.

EXAMPLES

Day 1 : Bullish Candlestick forms with the open at ₹50 , high at ₹58 , low at ₹46 and close at ₹56

Day 2 - Gap up open at ₹59 than market decline make lows of ₹48 and close at ₹50 covering 50% of bullish candle which show strong negative sentiment

UNIQUE INDEXES:

Apart from the main indexes like Sensex and Nifty, India has unique indexes such as the Nifty 100 ESG Index, which tracks companies with strong environmental, social, and governance practices.

ACTIVITY TIME

When a Dark Cloud Cover pattern formed on the daily chart of Birlasoft Ltd (stock name). How did the share react one weak after the formation ?

- Didn't reacted
- Rapidly move upward
- Rapidly gone down

TWEEZER BOTTOM & TWEEZER TOP CANDLESTICK PATTERN

PATTERN 5

TWEEZERS PATTERN

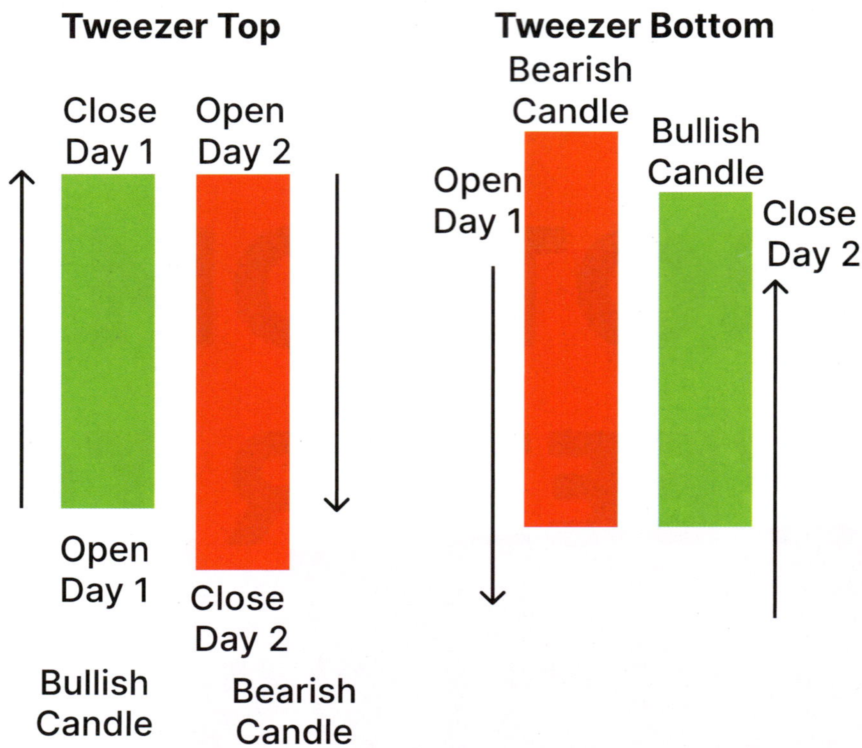

Tweezer Bottom और Tweezer Top candlestick patterns दो candlesticks से bante हैं और market के trend reversals को indicate करते हैं। Tweezer word Japanese ने एक tool से लिया है जिसको हम अपनी daily life में "chimti" के नाम से use karte हैं। ये patterns strong reversal signals देते हैं और trader को potential buying या selling opportunities दिखाते हैं।

CONCEPT

Tweezers candlestick pattern 12 तरीके के बन सकते हैं। मैं आपको concept समझाऊँगा ताकि ये 12 के 12 patterns आपको याद किए बिना ही detect करने आ जाएँ। एक बहुत ही simple concept है, अगर Tweezer bottom है तो दोनों candlesticks का bottom एक level पे होना चाहिए और अगर Tweezer top है तो दोनों का top same level पे होना चाहिए।

अब Tweezers में यही एक condition है कि Bottom Tweezer में bottoms same होने चाहिए और top Tweezer में tops. लेकिन ऐसा ज़रूरी नहीं है कि Bottom Tweezers में tops and Top Tweezers में bottoms same हो। अगर कभी दोनों ends same हो जाते हैं, along with shadows तो ये सबसे अच्छे and strong indication देने वाले Tweezers माने जाते हैं।

अगर Tweezer chart में नीचे की तरफ आता है तो वो Bullish trend (upward) indicate करता है और अगर chart में ऊपर की तरफ आए तो Bearish trend (downward).

TWEEZER BOTTOM

OVERVIEW:

Tweezer Bottom candlestick pattern एक bullish reversal signal है जो downtrend के बाद appear होता है। इस pattern में दो candlesticks होते हैं जो similar lows के साथ बनते हैं, और यह pattern downtrend को रोकने और possible uptrend शुरू होने का indication देता है।

STRUCTURE:

First Candlestick: एक लंबा bearish (red) candle जो strong selling pressure को दिखाता है।

Second Candlestick: Dusra candlestick bullish (green) candle होता है जो पहले candlestick के low के aas-paas ही close होता है, और similar low दिखाता है।

Note: 1st and 2nd candlesticks ke colour matter और sequence do not matter

MARKET PSYCHOLOGY:

Tweezer Bottom pattern market sentiment में shift को indicate करता है। पहले, sellers market को नीचे push करते हैं, लेकिन second candlestick ke दौरान buyers step in करके price को ऊपर push karte हैं और previous low को defend करते हैं। ये indicate करता है कि bulls strength gain कर रहे हैं और potential reversal हो सकता है।

EXAMPLE:

- Day 1: Bearish candlestick forms with the open at ₹50, high at ₹52, low at ₹46, and close at ₹48.
- Day 2: Bullish candlestick forms with the open at ₹50, high at ₹51, low at ₹48, and close at ₹51.

WHEN TO ENTER THE BUYING TRADE AND WHERE TO PLACE STOP LOSS:

- **Entry:** Traders might consider entering a buying trade after the close of Day 2, once the bullish reversal is confirmed. Entering the trade at the opening price of Day 3 or slightly above it could be a strategic entry point.
- **Stop Loss:** A prudent place to set the stop-loss could be below the low of the tweezer bottom, around ₹48 or slightly below it, to mitigate risk in case the reversal doesn't materialize.

SPOTTING THE TWEEZER BOTTOM PATTERN ON THE CHART:

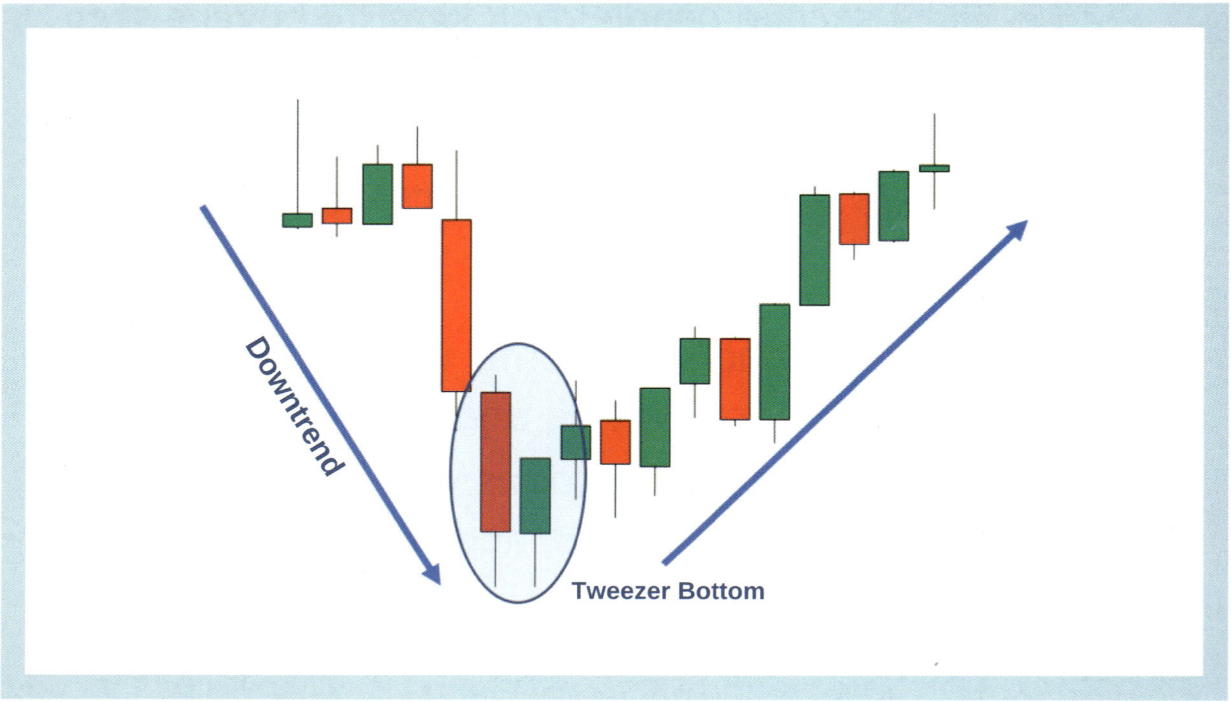

To spot the Tweezer Bottom pattern on the chart, look for two candlesticks with similar lows at the bottom of a downtrend. The first should be bearish and the second should be bullish, indicating a potential bullish reversal.

TWEEZER TOP:

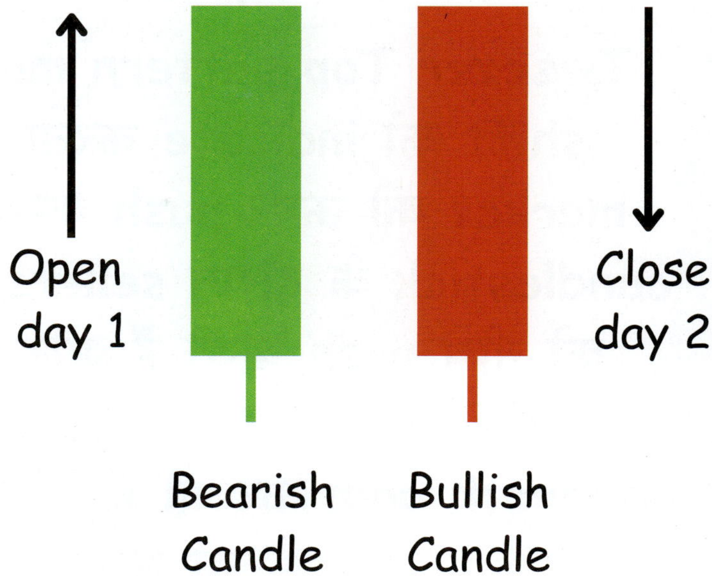

OVERVIEW:

Tweezer Top candlestick pattern एक bearish reversal signal hai jo uptrend के बाद appear होता है. इस pattern में do candlesticks hote hain jo similar highs ke saath bante hain, और यह pattern uptrend ko rokne और possible downtrend शुरू होने का indication deta hai.

STRUCTURE:

- First Candlestick: एक लंबा bullish (green) candle जो strong buying pressure को दिखाता है।
- Second Candlestick: Dusra candlestick bearish (red) candle होता है, जो पहले candlestick के high के आसपास ही close होता है, और similar high दिखाता है।

Market Psychology:

Tweezer Top pattern market sentiment में shift को indicate करता है। पहले, buyers market को ऊपर push करते हैं, लेकिन second candlestick के दौरान sellers step in करके price को नीचे push करते हैं और previous high को reject करते हैं। ये indicate करता है कि bears strength gain कर रहे हैं और potential reversal हो सकता है।

EXAMPLE:

- Day 1: Bullish candlestick forms with the open at ₹60, high at ₹63, low at ₹58, and close at ₹62.

- Day 2: Bearish candlestick forms with the open at ₹63, high at ₹64, low at ₹59, and close at ₹60.

TRADING

WHEN TO ENTER THE SELLING TRADE AND WHERE TO PLACE STOP LOSS:

- **Entry:** Traders may contemplate entering a selling trade after the close of Day 2, once the bearish reversal is confirmed. Entering the trade at the opening price of Day 3 or slightly below it could be a strategic entry point.

- **Stop Loss:** A strategic location to set the stop-loss could be above the high of the tweezer top, around ₹62 or slightly above it, to manage risk in case the anticipated reversal doesn't occur.

SPOTTING THE TWEEZER TOP PATTERN ON THE CHART:

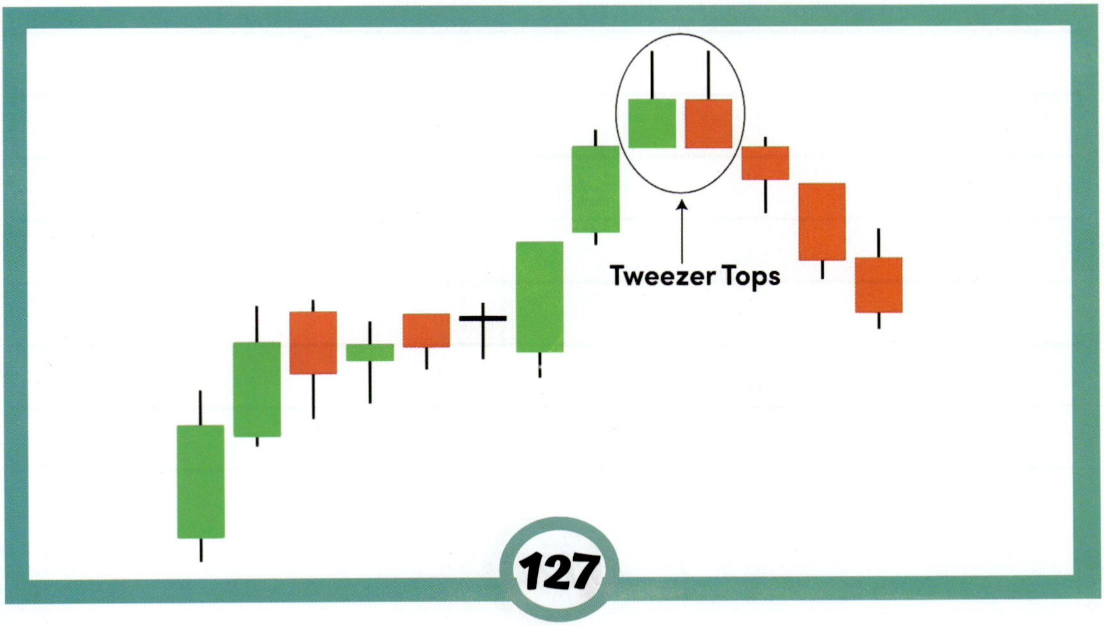

NOTES

NOTES

DID YOU KNOW? DID YOU KNOW? DID YOU KNOW

MARKET CAPITALIZATION AND GDP LINK:

Historically, the total market capitalization of BSE has hovered around 75-80% of India's GDP, but this number can fluctuate widely due to changes in investor sentiment and global economic conditions.

ACTIVITY TIME

Look at Kotak Mahindra Chart on 27th march 2022, A tweezer top was formed. Did the pattern coincide with any key support or resistance level ?

- Yes
- No

To Open Free Demat Account, Just Scan the QR Code

4.

Three & Three+ Candlesticks Patterns

MORNING STAR & EVENING STAR

PATTERN 1

MORNING STAR

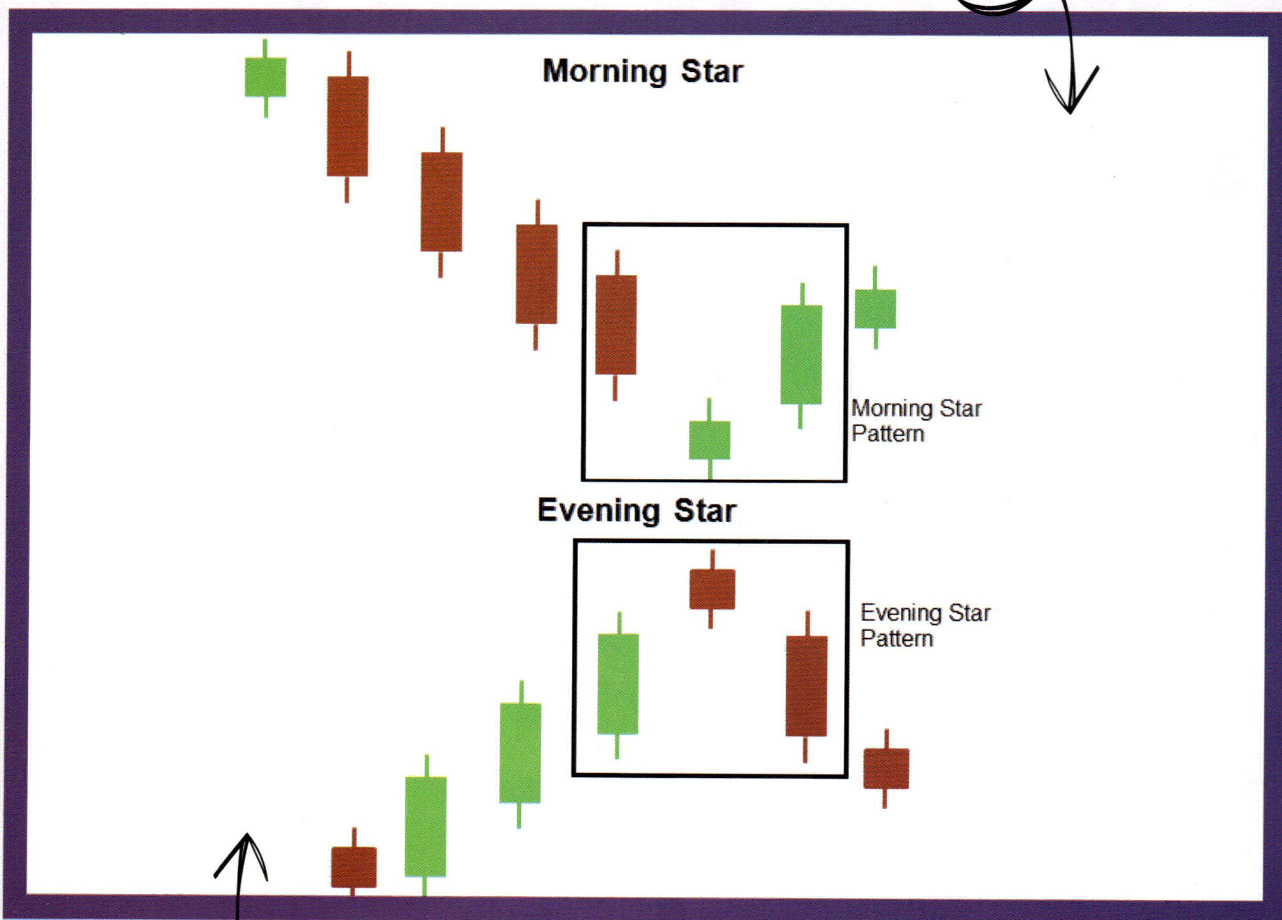

EVENING STAR

MORNING STAR:

OVERVIEW

Morning Star candlestick pattern एक bullish reversal signal है जो downtrend के बाद appear होता है। ये pattern three candlesticks से मिलकर बनता है और downtrend को रोकने और possible uptrend शुरू होने का indication देता है।

STRUCTURE

First Candlestick: एक लंबा bearish (red) candle जो strong selling pressure को दिखाता है।

Second Candlestick: एक छोटा candlestick (bearish या bullish/ Red या Green, doesn't matter) जो gap down के साथ बनता है, indicating indecision or consolidation.

Third Candlestick: एक लंबा bullish (green) candle जो पहले candlestick के body के mid-point के ऊपर close होता है, confirming the reversal.

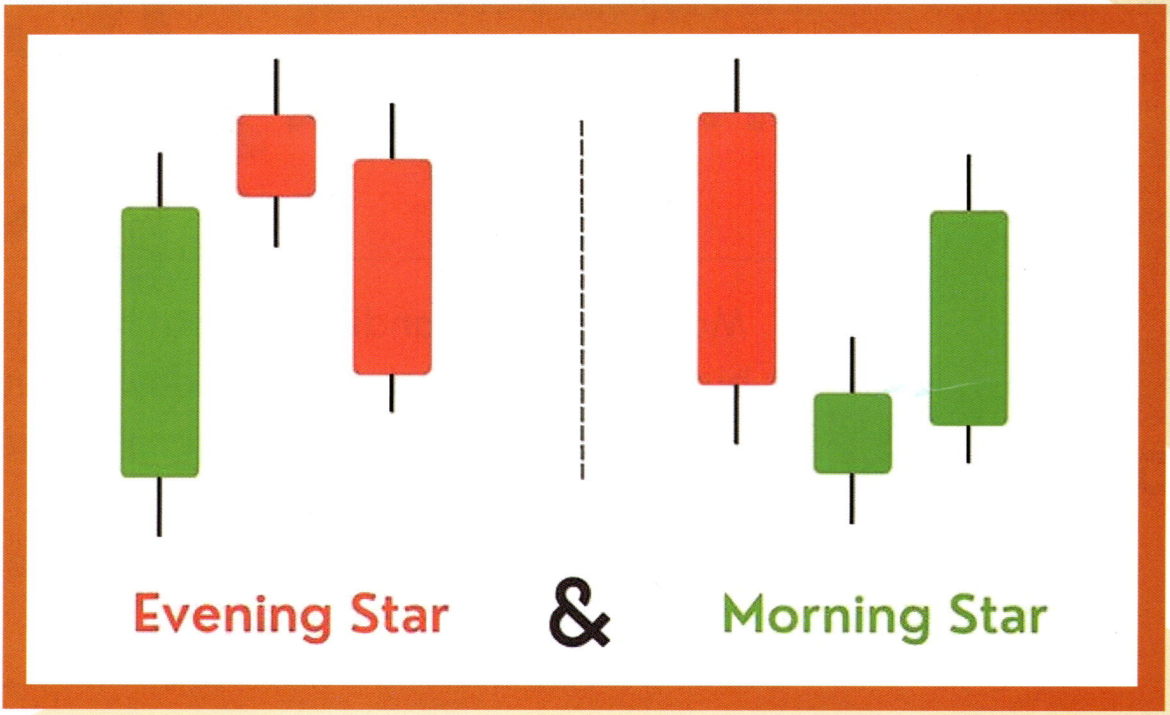

Note: हमें ये ध्यान में रखना होगा कि third candle first candle के high को break ना करे। हालांकि अगर high break हो भी जाता है तब भी ये pattern morning star का ही रहेगा, लेकिन फिर इस signal कि intensity कम हो जाएगी। First candle के high को break करने वाली candle fourth number पे आनी चाहिए। Isse bullish trend का काफी strong signal मिलेगा, जिससे we can confirm the potential uptrend.

MARKET PSYCHOLOGY:

Morning Star pattern market sentiment में shift ko indicate करता है। Pehle, sellers market को नीचे push करते हैं। दूसरा candlestick buyers और sellers के बीच fight को दिखाता है। Teesra candlestick buyers के dominance को दिखाता है, indicating a potential bullish reversal.

EXAMPLE:

- **Day 1:** Bearish candlestick forms with the open at ₹50, high at ₹52, low at ₹47, and close at ₹48.
- **Day 2:** Small candlestick forms with the open at ₹47, high at ₹48.5, low at ₹46.5, and close at ₹47.
- **Day 3:** Bullish candlestick forms with the open at ₹47.5, high at ₹50.5, low at ₹47, and close at ₹50.

WHEN TO ENTER THE BUYING TRADE AND WHERE TO PLACE STOP LOSS:

- **Entry:** Traders might consider entering a buying trade after the close of Day 3, once the bullish reversal is confirmed. Entering the trade at the opening price of Day 4 or slightly above it could be a strategic entry point.
- **Stop Loss:** A prudent place to set the stop-loss could be below the low of the pattern, around ₹46 or slightly below it, to mitigate risk in case the reversal doesn't materialize.

SPOTTING THE MORNING STAR PATTERN ON THE CHART:

- Stop Loss: A prudent place to set the stop-loss could be below the low of the pattern, around ₹46 or slightly below it, to mitigate risk in case the reversal doesn't materialize.

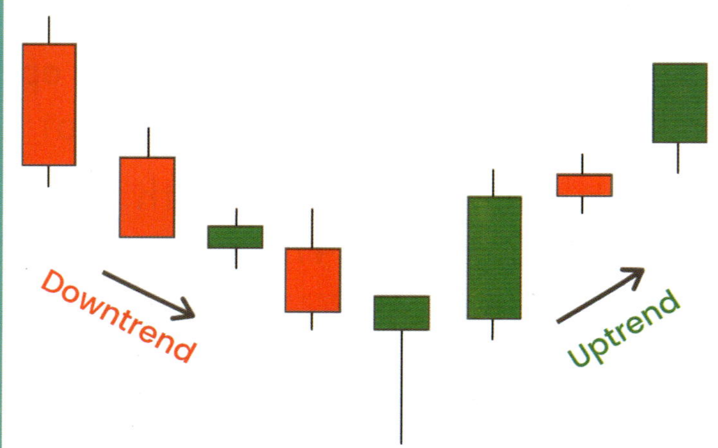

HAMMER CANDLESTICK

To spot the Morning Star pattern on the chart, look for a sequence of three candlesticks: a long bearish candlestick, followed by a small candlestick (indicating indecision), and then a long bullish candlestick. This pattern is found at the bottom of a downtrend, indicating a potential bullish reversal.

EVENING STAR:

OVERVIEW

Evening Star candlestick pattern एक bearish reversal signal है जो uptrend के बाद appear होता है। ये pattern three candlesticks से मिलकर बनता है और uptrend को रोकने और possible downtrend शुरू होने का indication देता है।

STRUCTURE

First Candlestick: एक लंबा bullish (green) candle जो strong buying pressure को दिखाता है।

Second Candlestick: एक छोटा candlestick (bullish ya bearish) जो gap up के साथ बनता है, indicating indecision or consolidation.

Third Candlestick: एक लंबा bearish (red) candle जो पहले candlestick ke body के mid-point के नीचे close होता है, confirming the reversal

MARKET PSYCHOLOGY:

Evening Star pattern market sentiment में shift को indicate करता है। पहले, buyers market को ऊपर push करते हैं। दूसरा candlestick buyers और sellers के बीच fight को दिखाता है। तीसरा, candlestick सेलर्स के dominance को दिखाता है, indicating a potential bearish reversal.

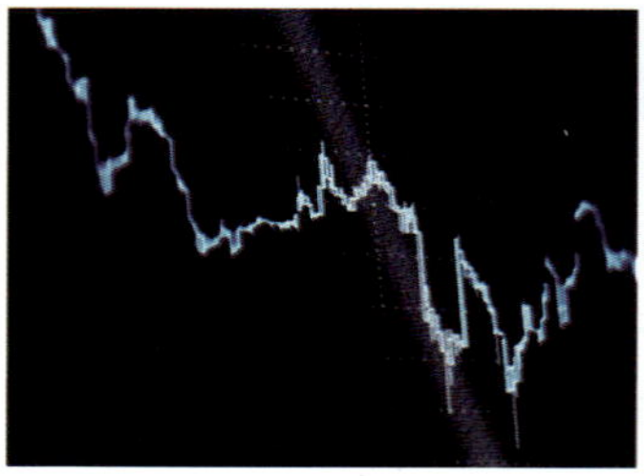

EXAMPLE:

- Day 1: Bullish candlestick forms with the open at ₹60, high at ₹62, low at ₹58, and close at ₹62.
- Day 2: Small candlestick forms with the open at ₹63, high at ₹64, low at ₹62.5, and close at ₹63.
- Day 3: Bearish candlestick forms with the open at ₹62.5, high at ₹63, low at ₹59.5, and close at ₹60.

WHEN TO ENTER THE SELLING TRADE AND WHERE TO PLACE STOP LOSS:

- **Entry:** Traders may contemplate entering a selling trade after the close of Day 3, once the bearish reversal is confirmed. Entering the trade at the opening price of Day 4 or slightly below it could be a strategic entry point.
- **Stop Loss:** A strategic location to set the stop-loss could be above the high of the pattern, around ₹64 or slightly above it, to manage risk in case the anticipated reversal doesn't occur.

SPOTTING THE EVENING STAR PATTERN ON THE CHART:

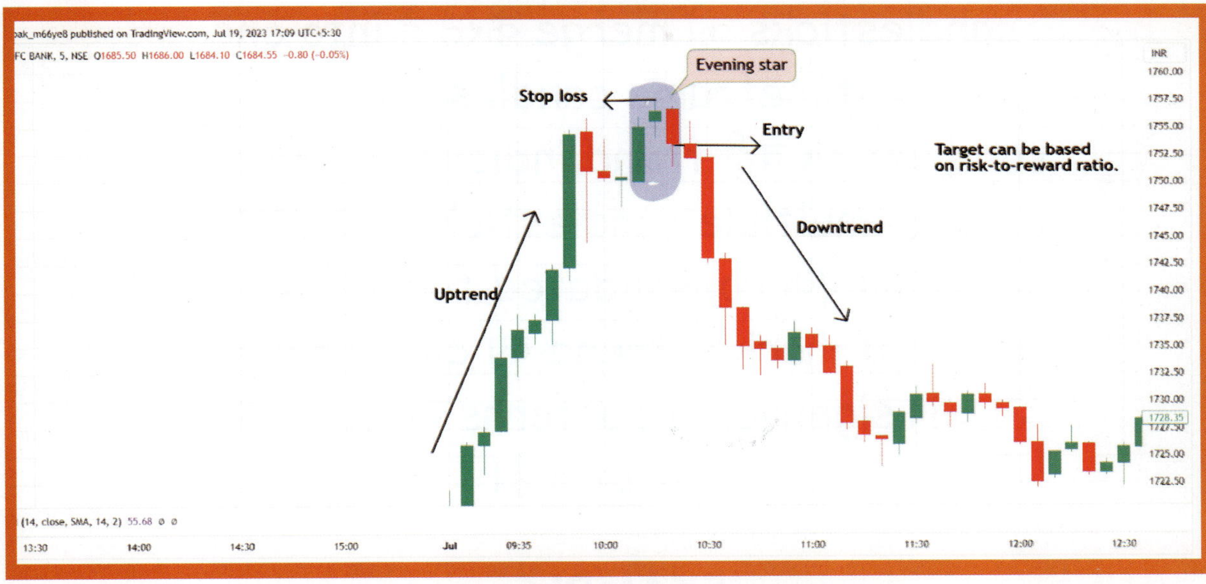

To spot the Evening Star pattern on the chart, look for a sequence of three candlesticks: a long bullish candlestick, followed by a small candlestick (indicating indecision), and then a long bearish candlestick. This pattern is found at the top of an uptrend, indicating a potential bearish reversal. These patterns help traders identify potential reversals in market trends and make more informed trading decisions.

MERGING CANDLESTICK PATTERNS:

जब हम multiple shorter-timeframe candlesticks को merge करते हैं into one longer-timeframe candlestick, तो नया candlestick वही trend indication देता है jo original multiple candlesticks दे रहे होते हैं, लेकिन एक consolidated form में। ये concept market trend का clearer view देने और significant patterns को spot करने में helpful है।

EXAMPLE:

MERGING 3 FIVE-MINUTE CANDLESTICKS INTO ONE FIFTEEN-MINUTE CANDLESTICK

Chalo consider करते हैं 3 five-minute candlesticks को merge करके एक fifteen-minute candlestick बनाते हैं। ये combined candlestick वही trend indication देगा जो 3 individual candlesticks दे रहे हैं, लेकिन simplified form में।

STEPS TO MERGE CANDLESTICK

4

3

Determine the Low Price: Naye candlestick ka low price teenon candlesticks ke beech ka lowest price होता है.

2

Determine the High Price: नए candlestick का high price तीनों candlesticks के बीच का highest price होता है।

1

Determine the Close Price: नए candlestick का close price तीसरा candlestick के close price के barabar होता है।

Determine the Open Price: Naye candlestick का open price पहला candlestick के open price के barabar होता है।

EXAMPLE:

1

First 5-Minute Candlestick:

- Open: ₹100
- High: ₹102
- Low: ₹99
- Close: ₹101

2

Second 5-Minute Candlestick:

- Open: ₹101
- High: ₹103
- Low: ₹100
- Close: ₹102

3

Third 5-Minute Candlestick:

- Open: ₹102
- High: ₹104
- Low: ₹101
- Close: ₹103

MERGED 15-MINUTE CANDLESTICK:

- Open: ₹100 (पहला candlestick का open)
- High: ₹104 (highest high among three candlesticks)
- Low: ₹99 (lowest low among three candlesticks)

Close: ₹103 (teesra candlestick का close)

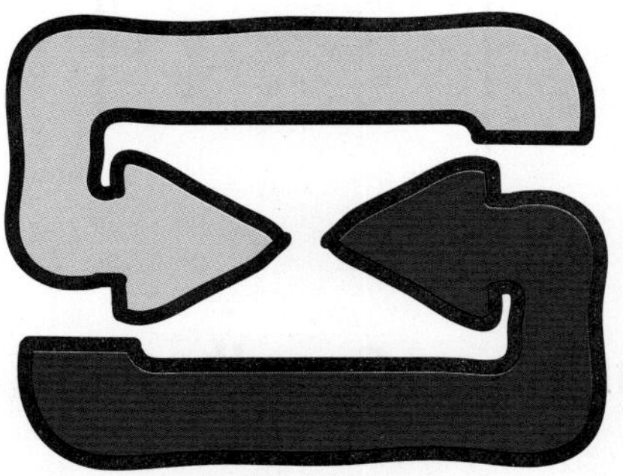

ये नया 15-minute candlestick bullish candlestick है जो upward momentum दिखाता है, बिल्कुल वैसे ही जैसे individual 5-minute candlesticks bullish trend indicate कर रहे हैं। हमारे इस three candlestick pattern को अगर merge करके single candlestick बनाया जाता तो, Bullish side में Hammer pattern बनता और Bearish side पे Shooting star.

HAMMER PATTERN:

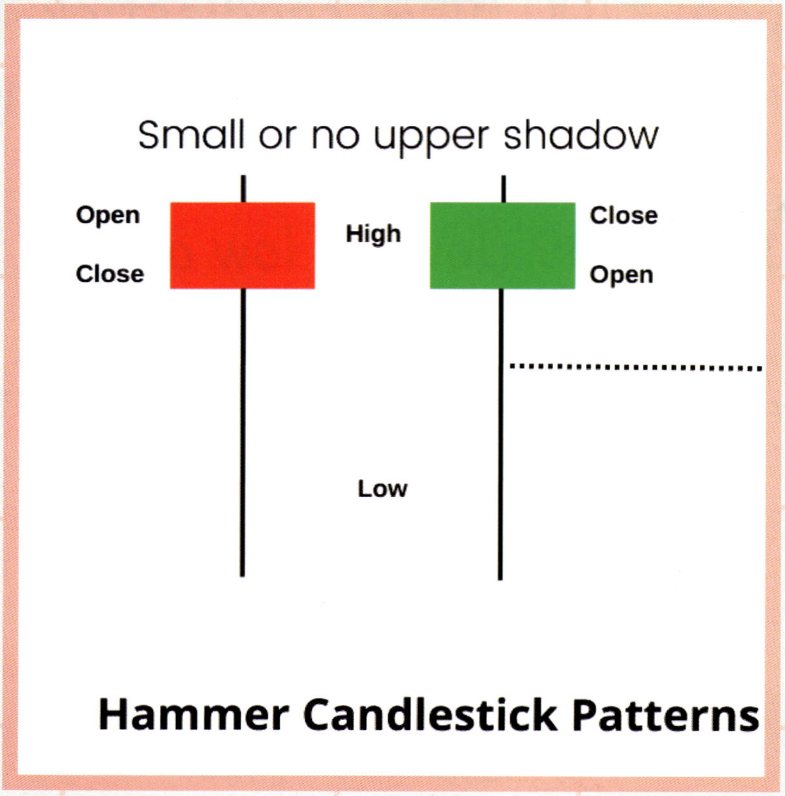

Hammer pattern downtrend में बनता है और एक potential bullish reversal indicate करता है। इसका long lower shadow और एक small real body होती है top पे।

EXAMPLE:

First 5-Minute Candlestick:

- Open: ₹50
- High: ₹51
- Low: ₹45
- Close: ₹48

Second 5-MinuteCandlestick:

- Open: ₹48
- High: ₹49
- Low: ₹47
- Close: ₹48.5

Third 5-Minute Candlestick:

- Open: ₹48.5
- High: ₹49
- Low: ₹47.5
- Close: ₹49

MERGED 15-MINUTE CANDLESTICK:

- Open: ₹50
- High: ₹51
- Low: ₹45
- Close: ₹49

ये merged candlestick long lower shadow और small body के साथ hammer जैसा लगता है और potential bullish reversal indicate करता है।

The hammer candlestick pattern is a bullish reversal signal that forms after a downtrend. It has a small body and a long lower shadow, at least twice the size of the body, indicating a potential price reversal. The short body suggests the bears pushed the price lower, but the bulls regained control. It appears at the bottom of a trend and is more significant when confirmed by higher volume and the following day's bullish price action. The upper shadow is either very short or nonexistent.

SHOOTING STAR PATTERN:

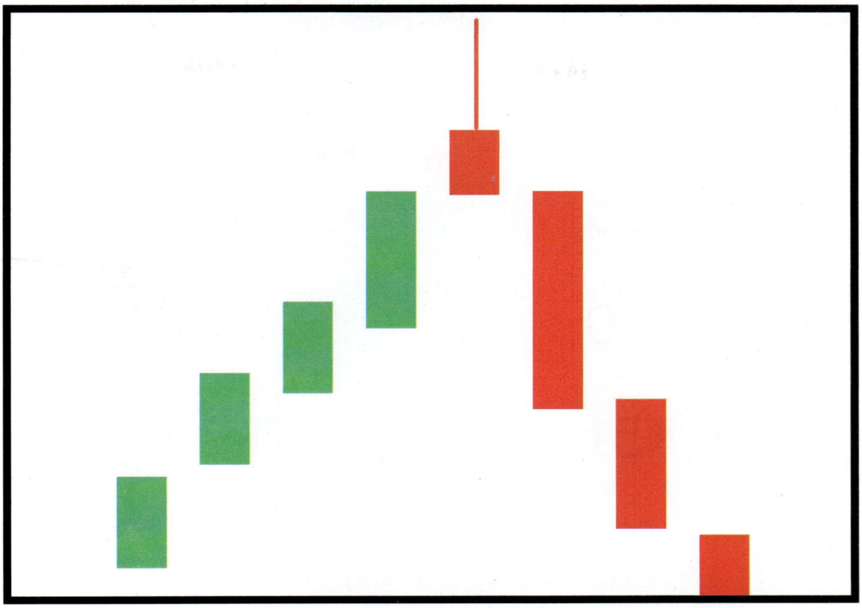

Shooting star pattern एक uptrend के बाद बनता है और एक potential bearish reversal indicate करता है। इसका long upper shadow और एक small real body होती है।

EXAMPLE OF MERGED SHOOTING STAR:

First 5-Minute Candlestick:

- Open: ₹50
- High: ₹55
- Low: ₹46
- Close: ₹46

SECOND 5-MINUTE CANDLESTICK:

Open: ₹52

High: ₹55

Low: ₹50

Close: ₹51

THIRD 5-MINUTE CANDLESTICK:

Open: ₹54

High: ₹57

Low: ₹54

Close: ₹54.5

MERGED 15-MINUTE CANDLESTICK:

Open: ₹50

High: ₹57

Low: ₹46

Close: ₹46

Ye merged candlestick long upper shadow और small body के साथ shooting star जैसा लगता है और potential bearish reversal indicate करता है।

ANOTHER EXAMPLE:

HAMMER PATTERN:

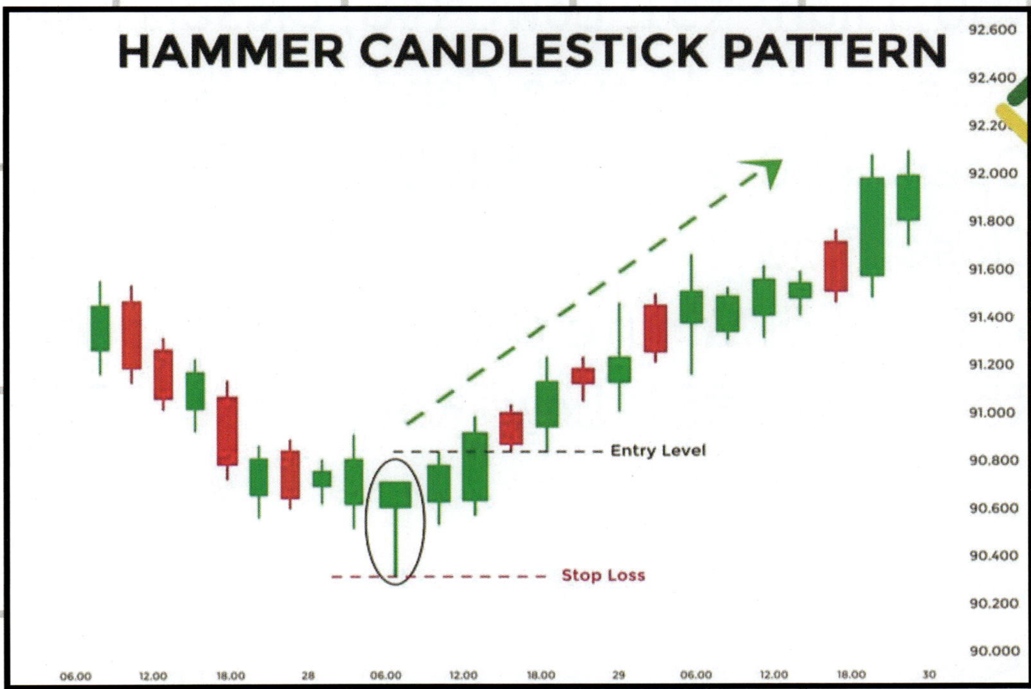

जब हम 3 five-minute candlesticks को merge करते हैं और वो सब same low price के around close होती हैं, तो एक Hammer बनता है। इसका open thoda upar close deta hai and low almost double hota hai body se .

EXAMPLE:

EXAMPLE

- First 5-Minute Candlestick: Open: ₹50, High: ₹51, Low: ₹48, Close: ₹50
- Second 5-Minute Candlestick: Open: ₹50, High: ₹51, Low: ₹48, Close: ₹50
- Third 5-Minute Candlestick: Open: ₹50, High: ₹51, Low: ₹48, Close: ₹50

Merged 15-Minute Dragonfly Doji: Open: ₹50, High: ₹51, Low: ₹48, Close: ₹50

GRAVESTONE DOJI FORMATION:

Gravestone Doji: जब हम 3 five-minute candlesticks को merge करते हैं और वो सब same high price के around close होती है, तो एक gravestone doji बनता है। इसका open, low और close price almost same होता है, बस high price एक sharp rise दिखाता है।

Example:

- First 5-Minute Candlestick: Open: ₹50, High: ₹52, Low: ₹50, Close: ₹51.5
- Second 5-Minute Candlestick: Open: ₹51.5, High: ₹53, Low: ₹51.5, Close: ₹52
- Third 5-Minute Candlestick: Open: ₹52, High: ₹54, Low: ₹52, Close: ₹53

Merged 15-Minute Gravestone Doji: Open: ₹50, High: ₹54, Low: ₹50, Close: ₹53

Multiple candlesticks को merge करना into one longer-time frame candlestick market trend का simplified और consolidated view provide करता है। ये technique significant patterns को easily identify करने और informed trading decisions लेने में madad करती है। Merging candlesticks के concept को समझकर, traders अपनी technical analysis skills को enhance कर सकते हैं और trend reversals को better spot कर सकते हैं।

The BSE lists over 5,500 companies, making it one of the largest in terms of the number of listings. The NYSE has around 2,400 listings, and NASDAQ about 3,600, but both markets host some of the world's most valuable companies, giving them much higher aggregate market value.

ACTIVITY TIME

On 26th Oct, 2021 an evening star Candlestick Pattern appeared on Daily Chart of Kotak Mahindra Bank. What was the subsequent Price Movement after that ?

- Correction of 17% to 18%
- No movement
- Strong upsidemove

BULLISH & BEARISH ABANDONED BABY

PATTERN 2

Bullish Abandoned Baby

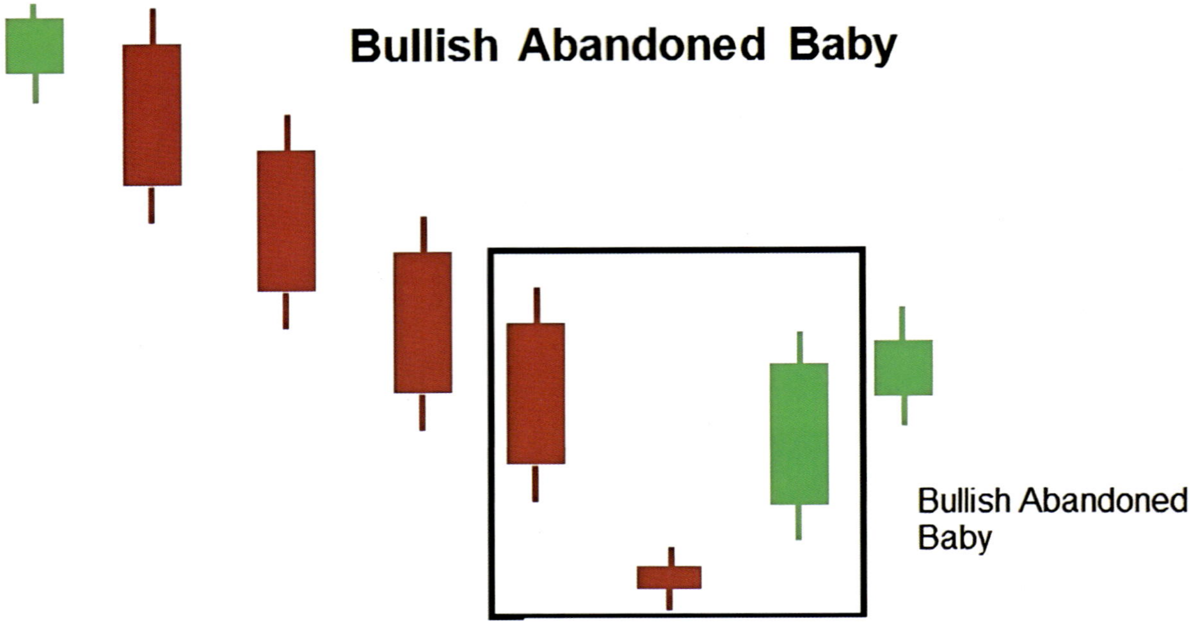

Bearish Abandoned Baby

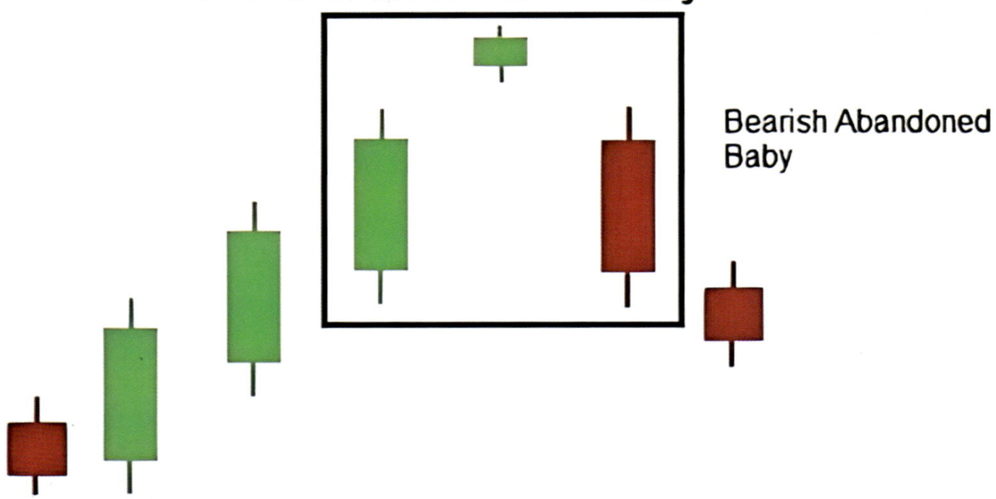

BULLISH ABANDONED BABY

जब एक downtrend के दौरान एक large bearish candlestick बनता है, उसके बाद एक doji candlestick होती है जो बड़े gap down के साथ open और close होती है, और फिर तीसरे दिन एक large bullish candlestick बनता है जो gap up के saath open होता है, तो यह एक bullish abandoned baby pattern होता है। यह pattern downtrend के खत्म होने और possible uptrend की shuruaat का indication देते हैं।

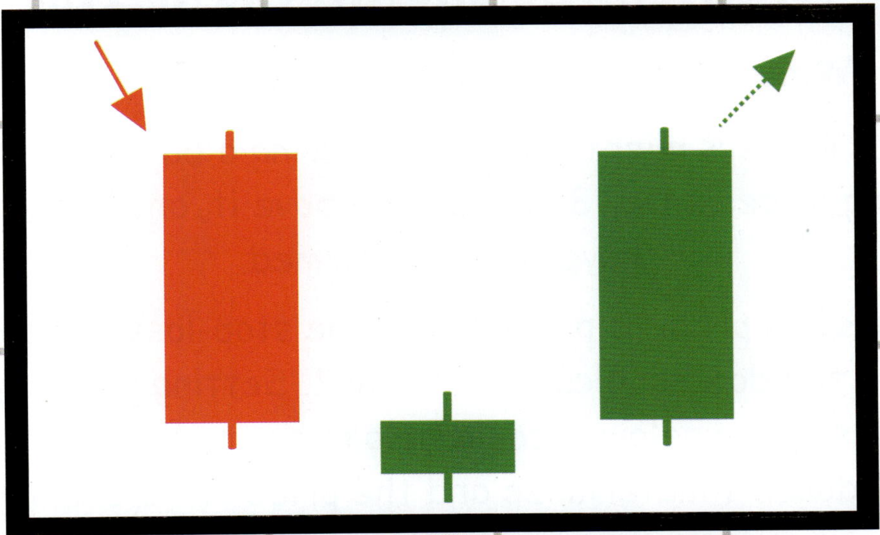

EXAMPLE:

DAY 1

A large bearish candlestick forms with the open at ₹50, high at ₹52, low at ₹48, and close at ₹48.

DAY 2

A doji candlestick forms with the open at ₹47, high at ₹47.5, low at ₹46.5, and close at ₹47.

DAY 3

A large bullish candlestick forms with the open at ₹49, high at ₹52, low at ₹48.5, and close at ₹51.

WHEN TO ENTER THE BUYING TRADE AND WHERE TO PLACE STOP LOSS:

- **Entry:** Traders might consider entering a buying trade at the opening price of Day 3 or slightly above it, once the bullish reversal is confirmed.
- **Stop Loss**: A prudent place to set the stop-loss could be below the low of the doji candlestick on Day 2. Setting the stop-loss at ₹46 or slightly below it could help mitigate risk in case the reversal doesn't materialize and the price turns bearish again.

SPOTTING THE BULLISH ABANDONED BABY PATTERN ON THE CHART:

To spot the bullish abandoned baby pattern on the chart, look for a large bearish candlestick followed by a doji candlestick that gaps down, and then a large bullish candlestick that gaps up. This indicates a potential bullish reversal.

BEARISH ABANDONED BABY

जब एक uptrend के दौरान एक large bullish candlestick बनता है, उसके बाद एक doji candlestick होती है जो gap up के साथ open और close होती है, और फिर तीसरे दिन एक large bearish candlestick बनता है जो gap down के साथ open होता है, तो यह एक bearish abandoned baby pattern होता है। यह pattern uptrend के khatam hone और possible downtrend की shuruaat का indication देता है।

EXAMPLE

A large bullish candlestick forms with the open at ₹60, high at ₹62, low at ₹58, and close at ₹62.

A doji candlestick forms with the open at ₹63, high at ₹63.5, low at ₹62.5, and close at ₹63.

A large bearish candlestick forms with the open at ₹61, high at ₹62, low at ₹59, and close at ₹60.

WHEN TO ENTER THE SELLING TRADE AND WHERE TO PLACE STOP LOSS:

- Entry: Traders may contemplate entering a selling trade at the opening price of Day 3 or slightly below it, once the bearish reversal is confirmed.
- Stop Loss: A strategic location to set the stop-loss could be above the high of the doji candlestick on Day 2. Setting the stop-loss at ₹64 or slightly above it could help manage risk in case the anticipated reversal doesn't occur and the price continues to rise.

SPOTTING THE BEARISH ABANDONED BABY PATTERN ON THE CHART:

To spot the bearish abandoned baby pattern on the chart, look for a large bullish candlestick followed by a doji candlestick that gaps up, and then a large bearish candlestick that gaps down. This indicates a potential bearish reversal.

DID YOU KNOW?

The abandoned baby is a rare but significant candlestick pattern that can be either bullish or bearish, signaling a strong potential reversal in the market. In a bullish abandoned baby pattern, it typically occurs after a downtrend. It consists of three candles: a large bearish candle followed by a small doji (a candle with little to no body), which gaps down from the previous candle, and finally, a large bullish candle that gaps up from the doji. The key feature of this pattern is the gaps on both sides of the doji, showing that the selling pressure has exhausted and buyers have taken control, signaling a reversal to an uptrend. In contrast, the bearish abandoned baby forms after an uptrend, starting with a large bullish candle, followed by a doji that gaps up, and then a large bearish candle that gaps down from the doji, signaling a potential reversal to a downtrend. The abandoned baby is a strong reversal signal due to the gaps, reflecting a sharp shift in market sentiment from one direction to the opposite.

Indian exchanges do not offer fractional share trading; investors must buy whole shares.while in USAFractional shares are widely available, especially through online brokers, making it easier for retail investors to own portions of high-priced stocks.

ACTIVITY TIME

What was the overall trend on the RBI Bank chart from August 21, 2024 to August 23, 2024. When a bearish abandoned baby pattern appeared?

- Downtrend
- Uptrend
- Sideway

THREE WHITE SOLDIERS & THREE BLACK CROWS

PATTERN 3

THREE WHITE SOLDIERS:

Three White Soldiers pattern एक bullish reversal signal है जो downtrend के बाद दिखाई देता है। इस pattern में, lagataar तीन bullish candlesticks बनती हैं जो trend reversal का indication देती हैं। हर candlestick पिछले candlestick के body के अंदर से open hoti है और high close पर khatam होती है, indicating a strong buying pressure.

EXAMPLE:

Day 1: A bullish candlestick forms with the open at ₹50, high at ₹54, low at ₹49, and close at ₹53.

Day 2: A second bullish candlestick forms with the open at ₹52, high at ₹56, low at ₹51, and close at ₹55.

Day 3: A third bullish candlestick forms with the open at ₹54, high at ₹58, low at ₹53, and close at ₹57.

WHEN TO ENTER THE BUYING TRADE AND WHERE TO PLACE STOP LOSS:

- **Entry:** Traders might consider entering a buying trade at the opening price of Day 4 or slightly above it, once the bullish trend is confirmed.
- **Stop Loss:** A prudent place to set the stop-loss could be below the low of the first bullish candlestick on Day 1. Setting the stop-loss at ₹49 or slightly below it could help mitigate risk in case the trend reversal doesn't materialize and the price turns bearish again.

SPOTTING THE THREE WHITE SOLDIERS PATTERN ON THE CHART:

To spot the Three White Soldiers pattern on the chart, look for three consecutive bullish candlesticks, each opening within the previous candlestick's body and closing near the high. This indicates a strong bullish reversal.

THREE BLACK CROWS

Three Black Crows pattern एक bearish reversal signal है जो uptrend के बाद दिखाई देता है। इस pattern में लगातार तीन bearish candlesticks बनती हैं जो trend reversal का indication देती हैं। हर candlestick पिछले candlestick के body के अंदर से open hoti है और low close पर खत्म होती है, indicating a strong selling pressure.

EXAMPLE:

Day 1: A bearish candlestick forms with the open at ₹60, high at ₹62, low at ₹56, and close at ₹58.

Day 2: A second bearish candlestick forms with the open at ₹57, high at ₹59, low at ₹54, and close at ₹55.

Day 3: A third bearish candlestick forms with the open at ₹54, high at ₹56, low at ₹52, and close at ₹53.

WHEN TO ENTER THE SELLING TRADE & WHERE TO PLACE STOP LOSS:

- **Entry:** Traders may contemplate entering a selling trade at the opening price of Day 4 or slightly below it, once the bearish trend is confirmed.
- **Stop Loss:** A strategic location to set the stop-loss could be above the high of the first bearish candlestick on Day 1. Setting the stop-loss at ₹63 or slightly above it could help manage risk in case the trend reversal doesn't occur and the price continues to rise.

SPOTTING THE THREE BLACK CROWS PATTERN ON THE CHART:

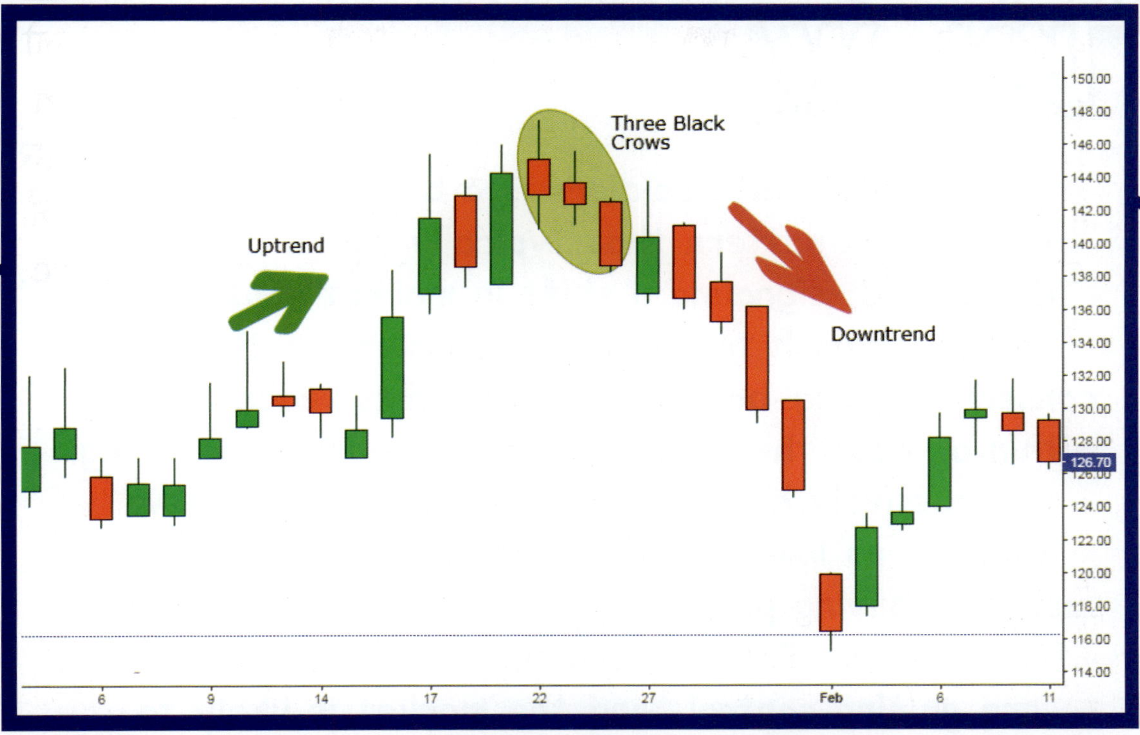

To spot the Three Black Crows pattern on the chart, look for three consecutive bearish candlesticks, each opening within the previous candlestick's body and closing near the low. This indicates a strong bearish reversal.

DID YOU KNOW?

The three white soldiers is a bullish reversal candlestick pattern that typically forms after a downtrend, signaling a shift in market sentiment from bearish to bullish. It consists of three consecutive long-bodied bullish candles, each opening within or near the previous candle's body and closing progressively higher. The candles generally have small or no lower shadows, indicating strong and sustained buying pressure, with little to no hesitation from sellers. This pattern suggests that the bulls are gaining control, and the market is likely to continue moving upward. Conversely, the three black crows is a bearish reversal pattern, appearing after an uptrend, where three consecutive long-bodied bearish candles form, each opening within or near the previous candle's body and closing progressively lower. This pattern indicates that selling pressure is strong and that the bears have taken over, signaling a potential continuation of the downtrend. Both patterns are regarded as reliable indicators of trend reversals when supported by other market factors.

Global Market Size: The global financial market is immense, with the combined stock markets of the world valued at over $100 trillion, while the bond market surpasses even that. The U.S. stock market alone represents around 40% of global market capitalization.

ACTIVITY TIME

On July 09, 2024 , A Three Black Crows Candlestick Pattern appeared on daily chart of Coforge ltd. Why this pattern failed choose the right one?

- Overall trend was bearish
- Overall trend was bullish
- Trend was Bullish and Pattern was formed near trendline

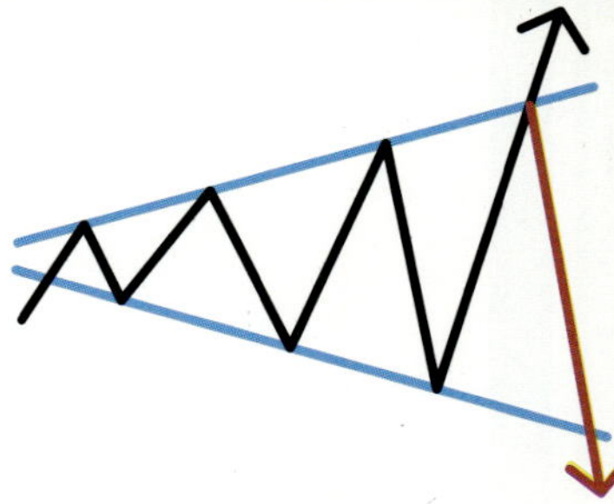

BULLISH & BEARISH THREE LINE STRIKE

PATTERN 4

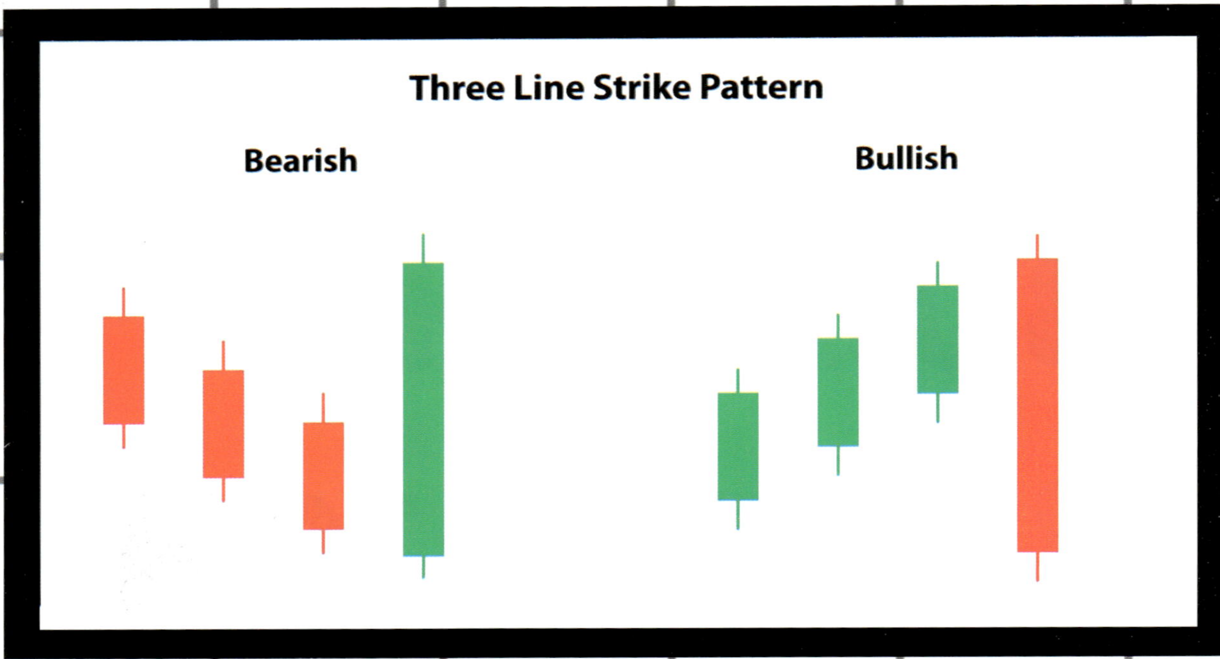

Three Line Strike candlestick pattern लगभग Three White Soldiers और Three Black Crows patterns के साथ similar होता है, लेकिन इसमें एक additional candlestick involved होता है, जो एक strong confirmation provide करता है और पहले के patterns को strike कर देते हैं।

BULLISH THREE LINE STRIKE:

Bullish Three Line Strike pattern एक bullish reversal signal है जो downtrend के बाद दिखाई देता है। इस pattern में लगातार तीन bearish candlesticks के बाद एक large bullish candlestick बनती है, जो पिछले तीन candlesticks के body और shadows को engulf करता है।

EXAMPLE:

Day 1: एक bearish candlestick बनता है जिसका open ₹50 है, high ₹52, low ₹48, और close ₹48.

Day 2: दूसरा bearish candlestick बनता है जिसका open ₹48 है, high ₹49, low ₹46, और close ₹47.

Day 3: तीसरा bearish candlestick बनता है जिसका open ₹47 है, high ₹48, low ₹45, और close ₹46.

Day 4: एक बड़ा bullish candlestick बनता है जिसका open ₹47 है, high ₹54, low ₹47, और close ₹53.

ENTRY और STOP LOSS:

- Entry: Traders को trading शुरू करने का विचार करना चाहिए। Day 5 के opening price पर ये उससे थोड़ा ऊपर, जब bullish trend confirm हो जाता है।
- Stop Loss: Stop-loss set करने का prudent स्थान Day 4 की fourth candlestick के low के नीचे हो सकता है। Stop-loss को ₹46 या उससे थोड़ा नीचे set करना risk को कम करने में मदद करेगा अगर trend reversal नहीं होता और price फिर से bearish हो जाती है।

BULLISH THREE LINE STRIKE PATTERN KO CHART PAR SPOTTING KAISE KAREIN:

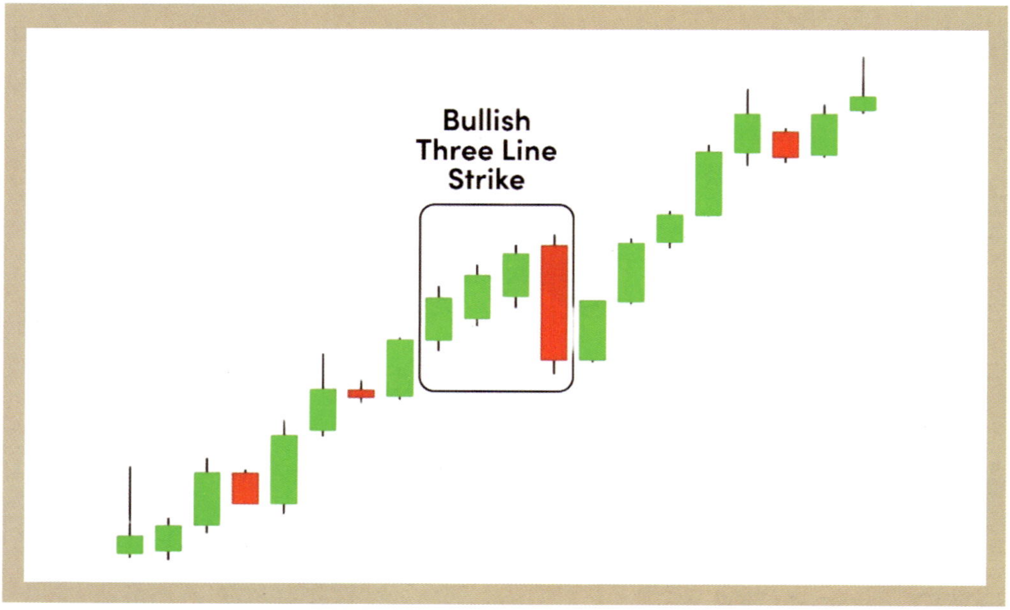

Bullish Three Line Strike pattern को chart पर spot करने के लिए तीन consecutive bearish candlesticks के बाद एक बड़ा bullish candlestick देखें जो पिछले तीन candlesticks के body और shadows को engulf करता है, तो यह एक strong bullish reversal को दर्शाता है।

BEARISH THREE LINE STRIKE:

Bearish Three Line Strike pattern एक bearish reversal signal है जो uptrend के बाद दिखाई देता है। इस pattern में लगातार तीन bullish candlesticks followed by एक large bearish candlestick बनती है, जो पिछले तीन candlesticks के body और shadows को engulf करता है।

EXAMPLE:

Day 1: एक bullish candlestick बनता है जिसका open ₹60 है, high ₹62, low ₹58, और close ₹62.

Day 2: दूसरा bullish candlestick बनता है जिसका open ₹62 है, high ₹64, low ₹60, और close ₹63.

Day 3: तीसरा bullish candlestick बनता है जिसका open ₹63 है, high ₹65, low ₹61, और close ₹64.

Day 4: एक बड़ा bearish candlestick बनता है जिसका open ₹64 है, high ₹65, low ₹58, और close ₹60.

ENTRY और STOP LOSS:

- Entry: Traders को trading शुरू करने का विचार करना चाहिए Day 5 के opening price पर या usse thoda नीचे, जब bearish trend confirm हो जाता है।
- Stop Loss: Stop-loss set करने का strategic स्थान Day 4 की fourth candlestick के high के ऊपर हो सकता है। Stop-loss को ₹65 या उससे थोड़ा ऊपर set करना risk को कम करने में मदद करेगा अगर trend reversal नहीं होता और price फिर से bullish हो जाती है।

BEARISH THREE LINE STRIKE PATTERN को CHART पर SPOTTING कैसे करें:

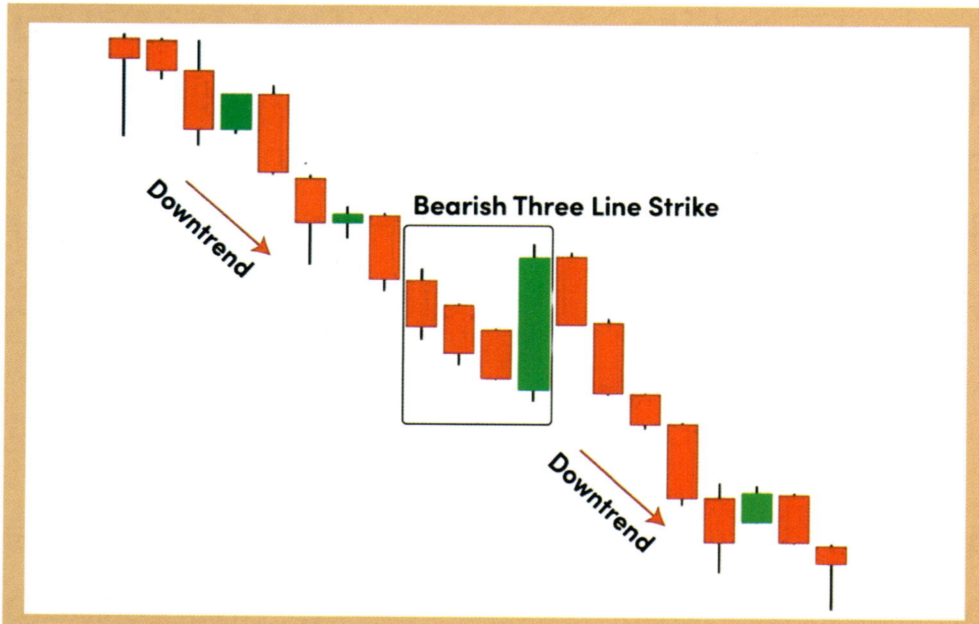

Bearish Three Line Strike pattern को chart पर spot करने के लिए तीन consecutive bullish candlesticks के बाद एक बड़ा bearish candlestick देखें जो पिछले तीन candlesticks के body और shadows को engulf करता है। यह एक strong bearish reversal को दर्शाता है।

NOW THIS PATTERN LOOKS SIMILAR TO TWO OTHER PATTERNS, BULLISH AND BEARISH ENGULFING PATTERNS AND THREE SOLDIERS AND CROWS. HERE IS HOW TO DIFFERENTIATE THEM:

KEY DIFFERENCES AND SIMILARITIES

- **Three Line Strike vs. Engulfing:**

  1. Three Line Strike: Requires three consecutive candles followed by a fourth opposite-direction candle that significantly reverses the previous three.

  2. Engulfing Pattern: Consists of only two candles where the second candle engulfs the first completely.

- **Three Line Strike vs. Three Soldiers/Crows:**

  1. Three Line Strike: The fourth candle is the key differentiator, providing a temporary reversal before the original trend continues.

  2. Three Soldiers/Crows: No fourth candle; the pattern focuses on three strong consecutive candles indicating a trend continuation or reversal.

DID YOU KNOW?

The three-line strike is a candlestick pattern that can either be bullish or bearish, signaling a potential reversal or continuation of a trend. In a bullish three-line strike, the market is in an uptrend, and three consecutive bullish candles are followed by a fourth large bearish candle that opens higher but closes below the first candle in the series. Despite the appearance of strong selling pressure, this pattern is considered bullish because it suggests that the market is "resetting" before continuing the upward trend. Conversely, in a bearish three-line strike, the market is in a downtrend with three consecutive bearish candles followed by a fourth large bullish candle that opens lower but closes above the first candle. Despite the bullish candle, the pattern is seen as bearish, signaling that the selling pressure may resume after a temporary rebound. Both patterns indicate market indecision, but they often predict that the prevailing trend will continue after the brief pause marked by the fourth candle.

ACTIVITY TIME

On 28th June 2024, a Bullish Three Line Strike Candlestick Appeared on Daily Chart Of Apollo Hospital Enterprise Ltd. What was Entry and Stoploss ?

- Entry Above 6217.75 (above forth candle high) and Stoploss 6070 (forth candle low ,fews point for buffer)

- At opening price of 5th day candle .

ACTIVITY TIME

The bearish 3 Line Strike candlestick pattern suggests a continuation of which trend ?

- Uptrend
- Downtrend
- Sideways

BULLISH & BEARISH THREE OUTSIDE UP & DOWN

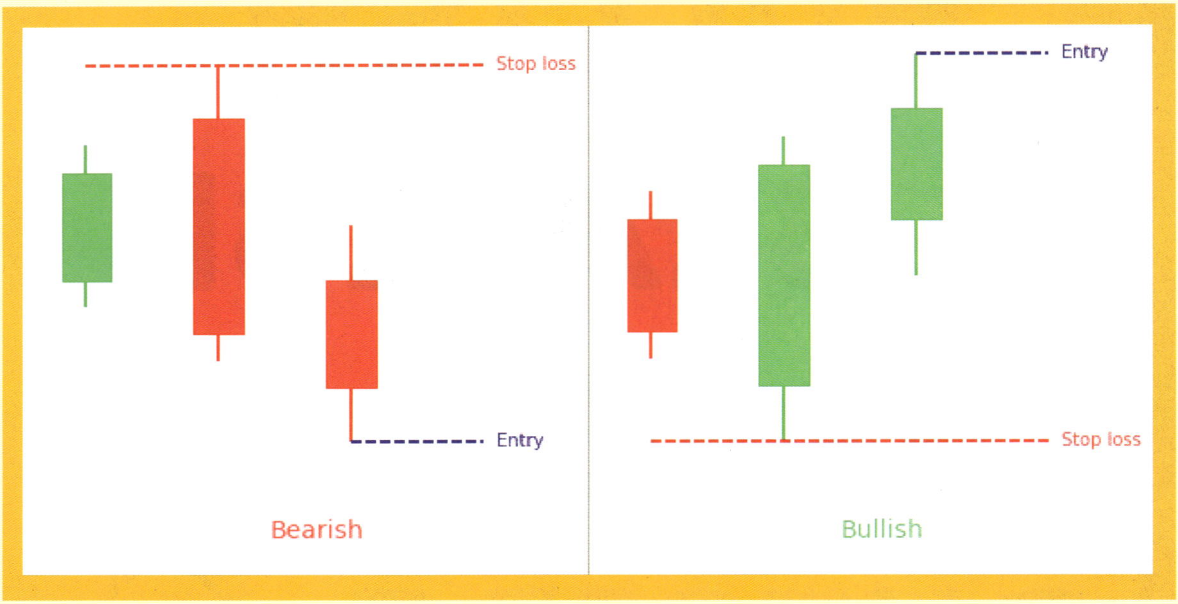

Three Outside Up और Three Outside Down candlestick patterns market में significant trend reversals को indicate करते हैं। यह patterns engulfing patterns से मिलते-जुलते हैं लेकिन तीनों candlesticks का sequence इन्हें unique बनाता है।

BULLISH THREE OUTSIDE UP:

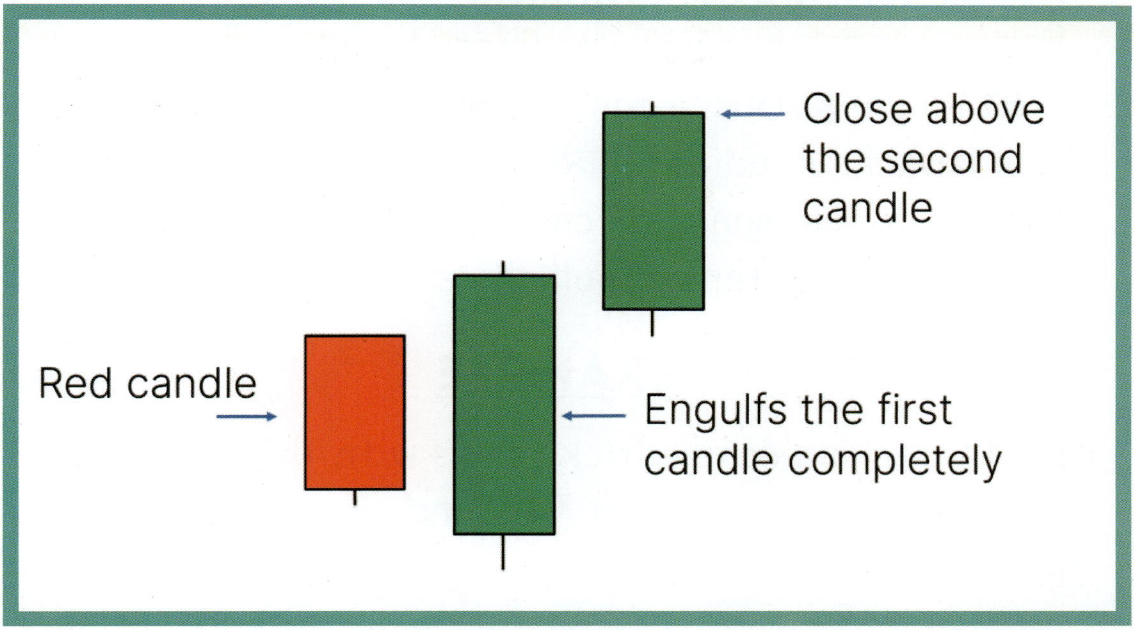

OVERVIEW:

Bullish Three Outside Up pattern एक bullish reversal signal है जो downtrend के बाद appear होता है। यह pattern three candlesticks से milkar बनता है और downtrend को rokne और possible uptrend शुरू होने का indication देता है।

STRUCTURE:

- **First Candlestick:** एक लंबा bearish (red) candle जो strong selling pressure को दिखाता है।
- **Second Candlestick:** एक लंबा bullish (green) candle जो पहले bearish candle को पूरी तरह engulf करता है।
- **Third Candlestick:** एक और bullish (green) candle जो second candle के close से ऊपर close होता है, confirming the bullish reversal.

MARKET PSYCHOLOGY:

यह pattern market sentiment में एक clear shift को दिखाता है। पहला bearish candlestick sellers के control को दिखाता है। Dusra candlestick buyers के strong comeback को indicate करता है और तीसरा candlestick buyers के dominance को confirm करता है, indicating a potential bullish reversal.

EXAMPLE

Day 1: Bearish candlestick forms with the open at ₹50, high at ₹52, low at ₹48, and close at ₹48.

Day 2: Bullish candlestick forms with the open at ₹47, high at ₹51, low at ₹46, and close at ₹50, engulfing Day 1's candlestick.

Day 3: Another bullish candlestick forms with the open at ₹50.5, high at ₹52, low at ₹49, and close at ₹51.

WHEN TO ENTER THE BUYING TRADE AND WHERE TO PLACE STOP LOSS:

- Entry: Traders might consider entering a buying trade after the close of Day 3, once the bullish reversal is confirmed. Entering the trade at the opening price of Day 4 or slightly above it could be a strategic entry point.

- Stop Loss: A prudent place to set the stop-loss could be below the low of the pattern, around ₹46 or slightly below it, to mitigate risk in case the reversal doesn't materialize.

SPOTTING THE BULLISH THREE OUTSIDE UP PATTERN ON THE CHART:

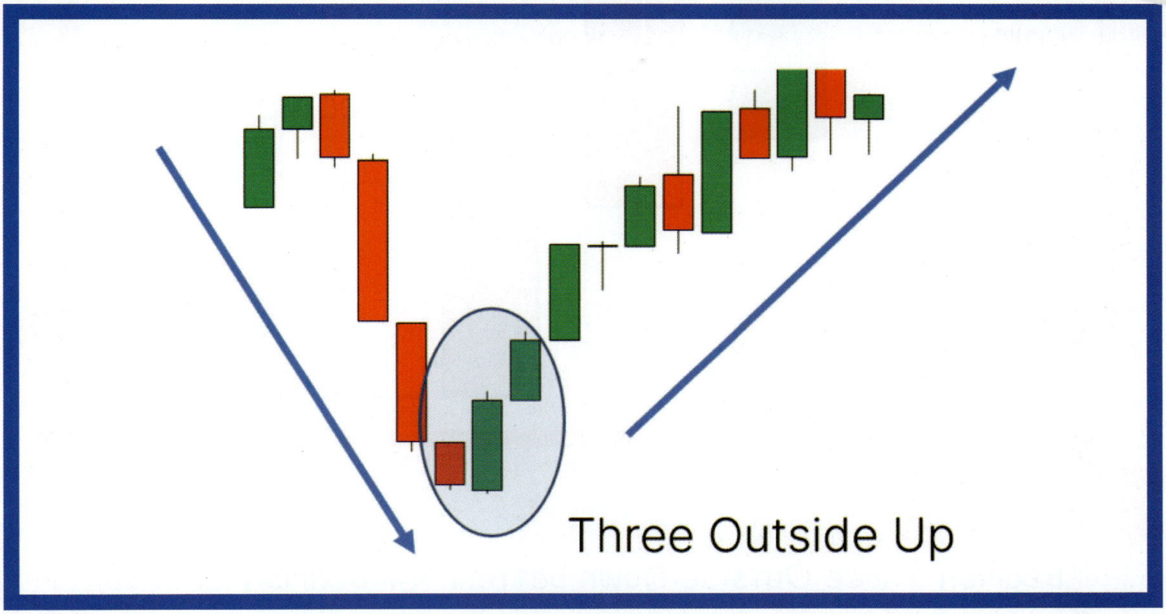

To spot this pattern on the chart, look for a sequence of three candlesticks: a long bearish candlestick, followed by a bullish candlestick that engulfs the first one, and then another bullish candlestick that confirms the reversal.

BEARISH THREE OUTSIDE DOWN:

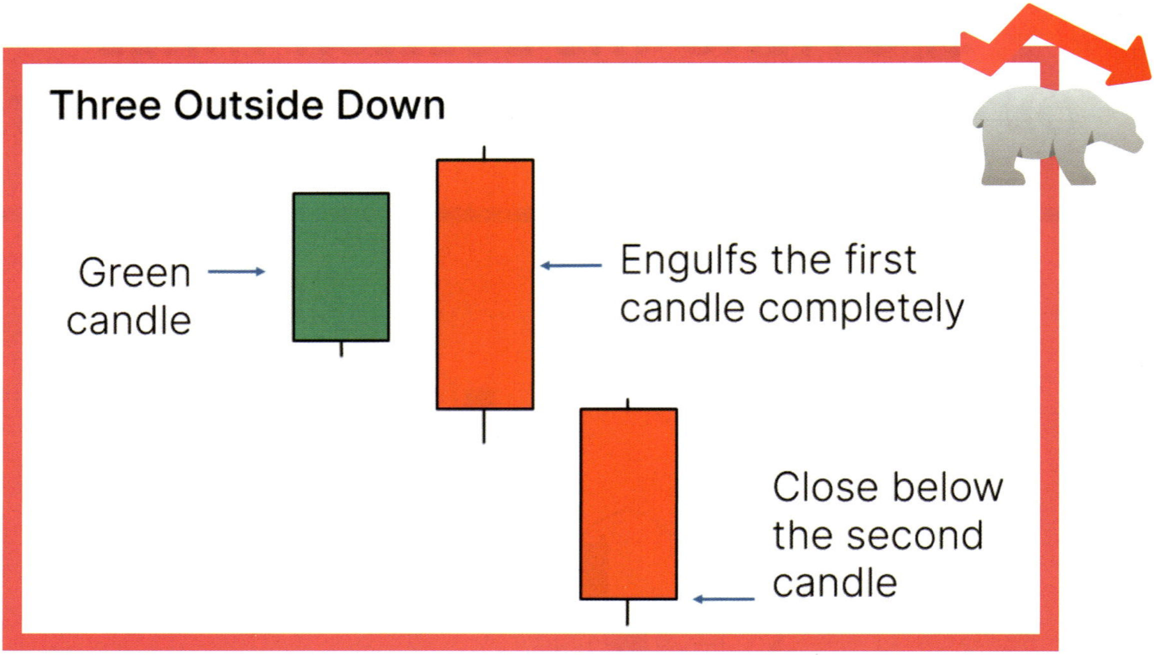

OVERVIEW:

Bearish Three Outside Down pattern एक bearish reversal signal है जो uptrend के बाद appear होता है। यह pattern three candlesticks से मिलकर बनता है और uptrend को रोकने और possible downtrend शुरू होने का indication देता है।

STRUCTURE:

1. **First Candlestick:** एक लंबा bullish (green) candle जो strong buying pressure को दिखाता है।

2. **Second Candlestick:** एक लंबा bearish (red) candle जो पहले bullish candle को पूरी तरह engulf करता है।

3. **Third Candlestick:** एक और bearish (red) candle जो second candle के close से नीचे close होता है, confirming the bearish reversal.

MARKET PSYCHOLOGY:

यह pattern market sentiment में एक clear shift को दिखाता है। पहला, bullish candlestick buyers के control को दिखाता है। दूसरा, candlestick sellers के strong comeback को indicate करता है और तीसरा, candlestick sellers के dominance को confirm करता है, indicating a potential bearish reversal.

EXAMPLE:

Day 1: Bullish candlestick forms with the open at ₹60, high at ₹62, low at ₹58, and close at ₹62.

Day 2: Bearish candlestick forms with the open at ₹63, high at ₹64, low at ₹60, and close at ₹59, engulfing Day 1's candlestick.

Day 3: Another bearish candlestick forms with the open at ₹58.5, high at ₹59, low at ₹56, and close at ₹57.

WHEN? TO ENTER THE SELLING TRADE AND WHERE TO PLACE STOP LOSS:

- **Entry:** Traders may contemplate entering a selling trade after the close of Day 3, once the bearish reversal is confirmed. Entering the trade at the opening price of Day 4 or slightly below it could be a strategic entry point.
- **Stop Loss:** A strategic location to set the stop-loss could be above the high of the pattern, around ₹64 or slightly above it, to manage risk in case the anticipated reversal doesn't occur.

SPOTTING THE BEARISH THREE OUTSIDE DOWN PATTERN ON THE CHART

To spot this pattern on the chart, look for a sequence of three candlesticks: a long bullish candlestick, followed by a bearish candlestick that engulfs the first one, and then another bearish candlestick that confirms the reversal.

DIFFERENTIATING OUTSIDE UP AND DOWN FROM SIMILAR PATTERNS:

ENGULFING PATTERNS:

- **Structure:** Two candlesticks where the second candlestick engulfs the first one completely.
- **Confirmation:** Immediate after the second candlestick, engulfing the previous one.

THREE LINE STRIKE:

- **Structure:** Three consecutive candlesticks in the direction of the trend, followed by a fourth candlestick that engulfs the previous three.
- **Confirmation:** The fourth candlestick provides a strong reversal signal by engulfing the previous three candlesticks.

THREE INSIDE UP AND DOWN

- **Structure:** Three candlesticks where the second candlestick fits entirely within the body of the first one, and the third candlestick closes beyond the range of the first candlestick.

- **Confirmation:** The pattern itself shows indecision and potential reversal with the confirmation coming from the third candlestick.

THREE OUTSIDE UP AND DOWN:

- **Structure:** Three candlesticks where the second candlestick engulfs the first one completely, and the third candlestick confirms the trend by closing beyond the range of the first two candlesticks.

- **Confirmation:** The pattern indicates a strong reversal with the confirmation coming from the third candlestick.

Currency Exchange Dominance: The Forex (foreign exchange) market is the largest in the world by trading volume, with an estimated $6.6 trillion traded every day, dwarfing the stock markets.

ACTIVITY TIME

On 22 May 23, a Bullish Three Outside Up candlesticks Pattern formed on daily chart of SBI LIFE INSURANCE CO LTD. Where you will not going to put stoploss ?

- below 5%
- below 2nd candle low
- will not going put stoploss

BULLISH & BEARISH THREE INSIDE UP & DOWN

PATTERN 6

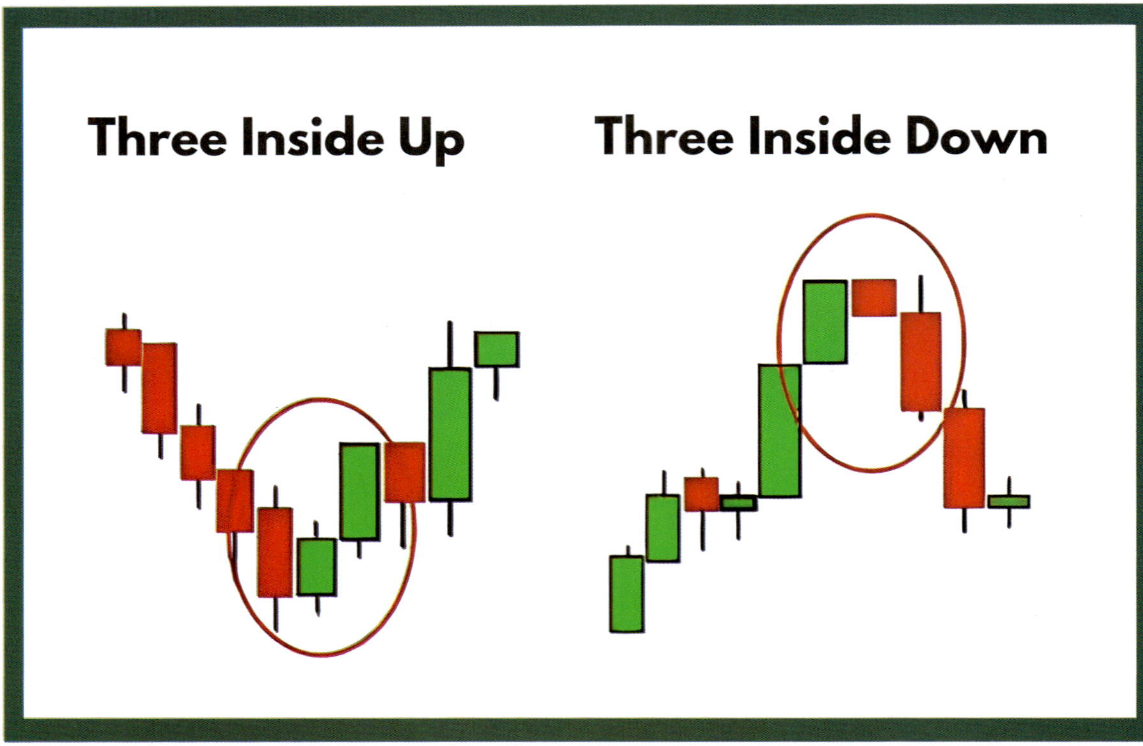

Inside Up और Inside Down candlestick patterns market में significant trend reversals को indicate करते हैं। यह patterns तीन candlesticks से मिलकर बनते हैं और एक particular trend के बीच में pause और फिर reversal को दिखाते हैं।

BULLISH INSIDE UP:

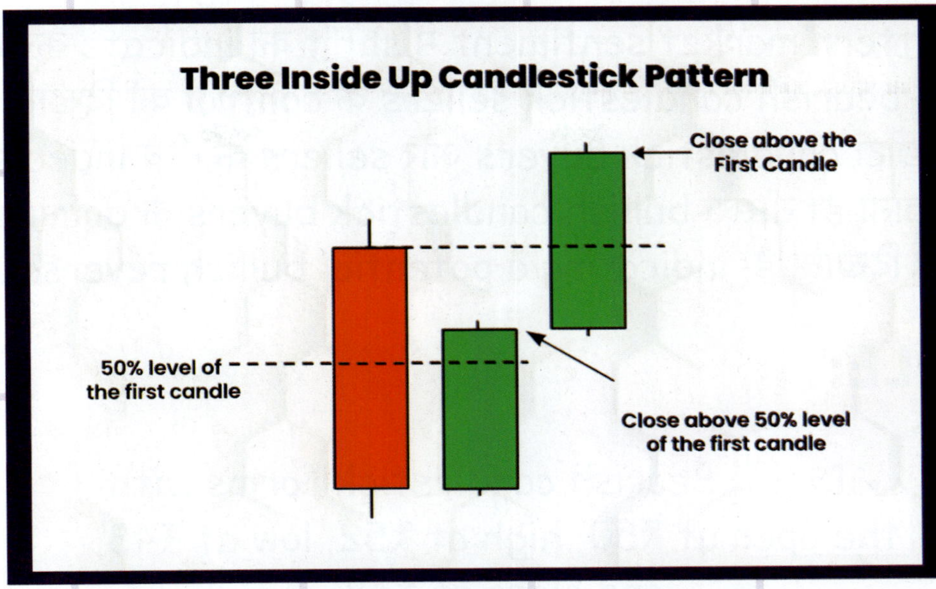

OVERVIEW:

Bullish Inside Up pattern एक bullish reversal signal है जो downtrend के बाद appear होता है। यह pattern तीन candlesticks से milkar बनता है और downtrend को रोकने और possible uptrend शुरू होने का indication देता है।

STRUCTURE:

- First Candlestick: एक लंबा bearish (red) candle जो strong selling pressure को दिखाता है।
- Second Candlestick: एक छोटा candlestick (red या green) जो पहले bearish candle के body के अंदर बनता है, indicating indecision or consolidation.
- Third Candlestick: एक लंबा bullish (green) candle जो पहले candlestick के high के ऊपर close होता है, confirming the reversal.

MARKET PSYCHOLOGY:

यह pattern market sentiment में shift को indicate करता है। पहला bearish candlestick sellers के control को दिखाता है। दूसरा छोटा candlestick buyers और sellers के बीच indecision को दिखाता है। तीसरा bullish candlestick buyers के dominance को दिखाता है, indicating a potential bullish reversal.

EXAMPLE:

- Day 1: Bearish candlestick forms with the open at ₹50, high at ₹52, low at ₹48, and close at ₹48.
- Day 2: Smaller candlestick forms with the open at ₹48.5, high at ₹49.5, low at ₹47.5, and close at ₹49, fitting entirely within the previous candlestick's body.
- Day 3: Bullish candlestick forms with the open at ₹49.5, high at ₹51.5, low at ₹49, and close at ₹51.

WHEN TO ENTER THE BUYING TRADE AND WHERE TO PLACE STOP LOSS:

- Entry: Traders might consider entering a buying trade after the close of Day 3, once the bullish reversal is confirmed. Entering the trade at the opening price of Day 4 or slightly above it could be a strategic entry point.

- Stop Loss: A prudent place to set the stop-loss could be below the low of the pattern, around ₹47.5 or slightly below it, to mitigate risk in case the reversal doesn't materialize.

SPOTTING THE BULLISH INSIDE UP PATTERN ON THE CHART:

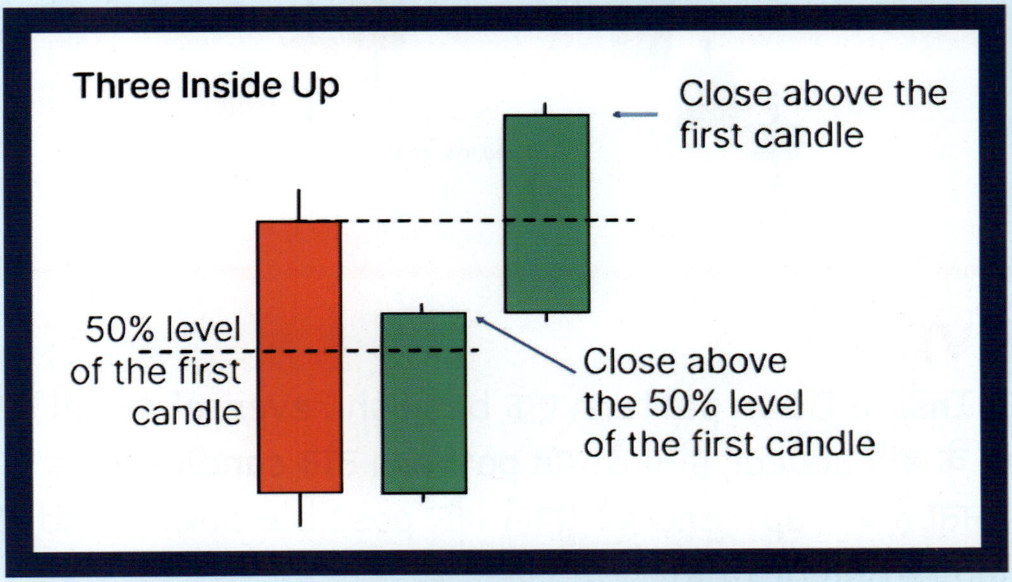

To spot this pattern on the chart, look for a sequence of three candlesticks: a long bearish candlestick, followed by a smaller candlestick that fits entirely within the body of the first candlestick, and then a long bullish candlestick that closes above the high of the first candlestick. This pattern is found at the bottom of a downtrend, indicating a potential bullish reversal.

BEARISH INSIDE DOWN:

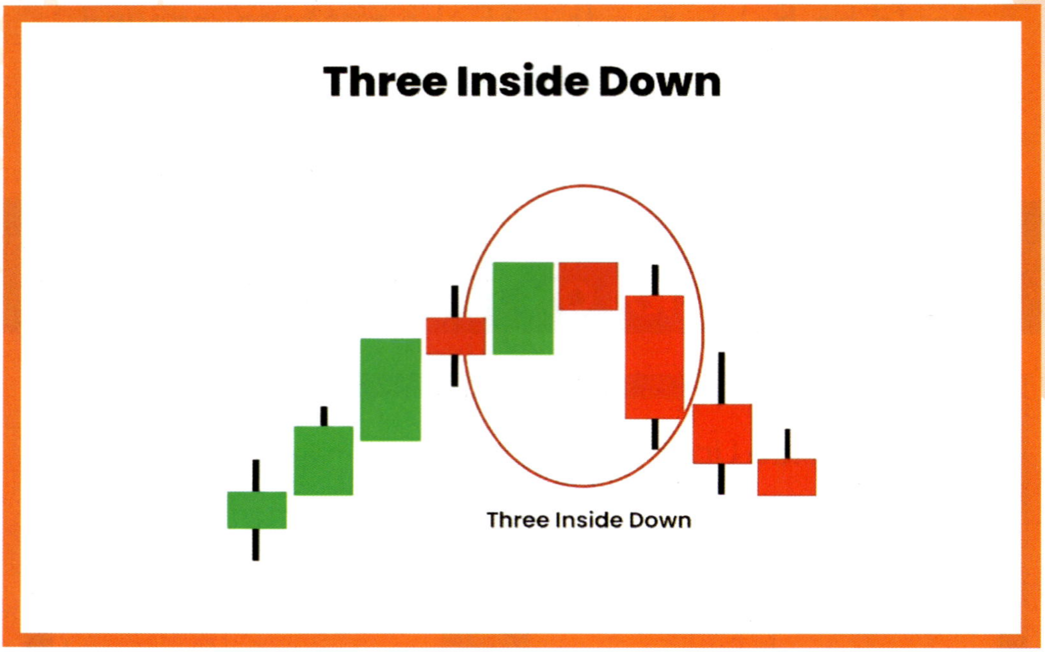

OVERVIEW:

Bearish Inside Down pattern एक bearish reversal signal है जो uptrend के बाद appear होता है। यह pattern तीन candlesticks से मिलकर बनता है और uptrend को रोकने और possible downtrend शुरू होने का indication deta है।

STRUCTURE:

- First Candlestick: एक लंबा bullish (green) candle जो strong buying pressure को दिखाता है।
- Second Candlestick: एक छोटा candlestick (green या red) जो पहले bullish candle के body के अंदर बनता है, indicating indecision or consolidation.
- Third Candlestick: एक लंबा bearish (red) candle जो पहले candlestick के low के नीचे close होता है, confirming the reversal.

MARKET PSYCHOLOGY:

यह pattern market sentiment में shift को indicate करता है। पहला bullish candlestick buyers के control को दिखाता है। दूसरा छोटा candlestick buyers और sellers के beech indecision को दिखाता है। तीसरा bearish candlestick sellers के dominance को दिखाता है, indicating a potential bearish reversal.

WHEN TO ENTER THE SELLING TRADE AND WHERE TO PLACE STOP LOSS:

- **Entry:** Traders may contemplate entering a selling trade after the close of Day 3, once the bearish reversal is confirmed. Entering the trade at the opening price of Day 4 or slightly below it could be a strategic entry point.

- **Stop Loss:** A strategic location to set the stop-loss could be above the high of the pattern, around ₹62.5 or slightly above it, to manage risk in case the anticipated reversal doesn't occur.

SPOTTING THE BEARISH INSIDE DOWN PATTERN ON THE CHART:

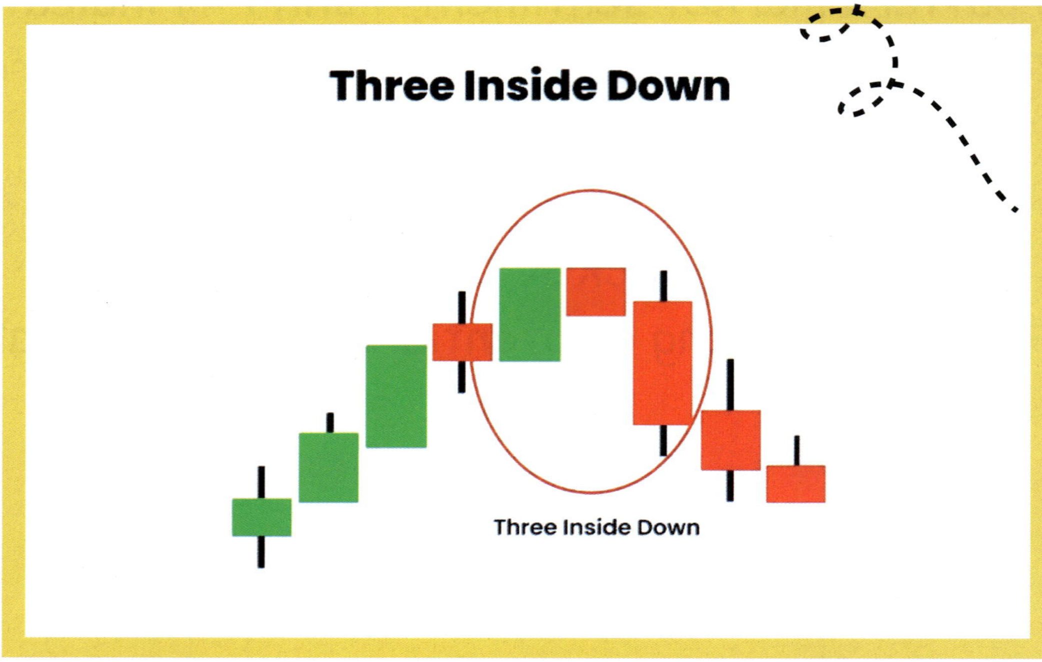

To spot this pattern on the chart, look for a sequence of three candlesticks: a long bullish candlestick, followed by a smaller candlestick that fits entirely within the body of the first candlestick, and then a long bearish candlestick that closes below the low of the first candlestick. This pattern is found at the top of an uptrend, indicating a potential bearish reversal.

DIFFERENTIATING INSIDE UP AND DOWN FROM SIMILAR PATTERNS:

ENGULFING PATTERNS:

- Structure: Two candlesticks where the second candlestick engulfs the first one completely.
- Confirmation: Immediate after the second candlestick, engulfing the previous one.

THREE LINE STRIKE:

- Structure: Three consecutive candlesticks in the direction of the trend, followed by a fourth candlestick that engulfs the previous three.
- Confirmation: The fourth candlestick provides a strong reversal signal by engulfing the previous three candlesticks.

INSIDE UP AND DOWN:

- Structure: Three candlesticks where the second candlestick fits entirely within the body of the first one, and the third candlestick closes beyond the range of the first candlestick.
- Confirmation: The pattern itself shows indecision and potential reversal with the confirmation coming from the third candlestick.

In summary, Bullish Inside Up and Bearish Inside Down patterns offer clear reversal signals with a distinctive three-candlestick structure. These patterns are distinct from other reversal patterns due to their unique structure of consolidation within the body of a single candlestick followed by a strong reversal, providing traders with early signs of market sentiment shifts.

NOTES

NOTES

U.S. DOLLAR SUPREMACY:

The U.S. dollar is involved in nearly 88% of all foreign exchange transactions, underscoring its position as the world's primary reserve currency.

ACTIVITY TIME

What does a bullish inside up candlestick pattern signify in terms of potential market trend reversal ?

- A continuation of the existing Downward
- A possible reversal from a downtrend to an uptrend
- A neutral market with no trend change
- Increase volatility with no clear trend direction